# The 21ST Century Complete Guide To Strippers

## Everything you need to know about Strippers, Gentlemen's Clubs and More!

By Mark Gorge

# *Mark Gorge's*
# *21st Century Guide to*
# *Strippers*

# Everything you need to know about Strippers, Gentlemen's Clubs and More!

**The author is available for consulting on all matters related to Gentlemen's Clubs and may be contacted initially via email at Mark@paymentsinfo.com**

**1st Edition – Amazon  Kindle Direct Publishing 2016**

**Library of Congress Catalog in-Publication Data**

Gorge, Mark, S

  The 21st Century Guide to Strippers/Mark Gorge

  ISBN:1535012366

  1. Strippers  2.Gentelmens Club's  3. Pornography

# Introduction

I want to start off by stating that this book isn't intended to upset anyone's moral beliefs. Irrespective of your personal outlook on the business of Strip Clubs, Strippers and everything related, it exists and will continue to. I hope you find this book entertaining and educational. If your thinking about becoming a stripper, opening a club, are curious about the inner workings of the business, are thinking or are curious about dating a stripper or just like a good story you bought the right book. Enjoy!

I led a pretty sheltered life, at least up to a point. I grew up in a pretty normal household in the suburbs of Detroit, Michigan in a city called Oak Park. The city of Oak Park was a dry city up until 2013 where after 60 years the city approved the sale of beer and wine by the glass. In 2015 Oak Park finally allowed the sale of harder alcohol. There were never any Strip Clubs in Oak Park. The city's south border is the infamous 8 Mile Road. Eight Mile road also known as M-102 runs east and west, starting at Vernier Road / I-94 in Harper Woods to the east. Going to the west it ends at Grand River in Novi. Eight Mile has always had the distinction of dissecting the City of Detroit and it's urban activities with the more affluent suburbs to its north. Located on Eight mile road within close proximity to where I grew up were multiple strip clubs . It was just a matter of time before I ended up in one.

Many people's first exposure to a strip club was via the 1982 Movie Porky's. It was the 5th highest grossing film of 1982 making about $111,000,000 . The plot revolved around some kids trying to lose their virginity in a strip club and their adventure. Prior to that,  in 1979 the movie Hardcore written and directed by Paul Schrader who was best known for writing  Martin Scoreses's, Taxi Driver gave people a taste of the adult entertainment industry. There were always stories about clubs and sex shows in Tijuana, Mexico. My grandparents generation grew up with Burlesque. In American history there are all kinds of references to "Dance Halls" in frontier towns. Most veterans of the military have stories about "Entertainment " while on leave. Bachelor parties and Stags have happened forever. Thus this industry is nothing new. It just seems to have evolved as do many other industries and vices embracing modern technology and current culture. I have seen extensive change in the past 30 years. Even  with this change and reflecting back historically the common denominator is *that men like to interact with women.* There seems to be a new trend that women and couples also like strip clubs. This probably isn't really new, it's just becoming more acceptable.

My first visit to a strip club was with some friends from the race track. During the summer of 1978 I was very involved with racehorses. I had just graduated from high school and was really enjoying my life. My day consisted of getting up around 5:30 am and taking care of my horses. When I refer to "my" horses, some were my responsibility in the scope of my work as a groom for other trainers and other horses were horses I owned or leased or trained for other people. Depending on what had to be accomplished that day, I typically finished up my work mid afternoon. Horses are usually fed around 4pm in the afternoon. I had an arrangement with people I knew at the track that on certain days I would feed and water their horses in exchange for them taking care of my horses other days. This task of feeding consisted of grabbing a water hose and filling up all of the horses water buckets. It was summer, hot and the horses drank a lot of water. Then throwing a few flakes of hay to each horse that had been previously set out. A flake is a fractional part of a bale of hay. About the size of a pizza box but twice as thick. And finally taking a coffee can of grain and giving it to horse in their feed pail. It went pretty quickly but had to be done. On the days I was at the track in the afternoon I also picked up my stalls. This means if the horse went to the bathroom since the morning when the stall was cleaned, and the always did, you picked it up with a pitch fork making your work in the morning a little easier and keeping the stall cleaner and the flies down. This routine of feeding was repeated again at night, usually after the races were over. Because during the races there was all kinds of activity. Horses going back and forth to the race track from the barn area. The announcer calling races. Trucks coming and going picking up and dropping off horses... I know this book is about strippers , not horses I'll get to the point soon. So I was very involved with horses and because of this I had some pretty good information about what was going on. I'd go up to the races most nights and eventually became pretty close with some of the biggest gamblers in the city. They liked what I knew and it developed into my routine to come up to the races, sit down, have a little dinner and talk horses. After the races I was always invited out with the guys. In 1978 there were no casinos in Detroit at least no legal ones. There were many "After Hours" places that opened up around 2:30 am after the bars closed. Of course these places were not legal but you could drink, gamble, and partake in most vices. Most of the places had fruit machines. These were a cross between a slot machine and a video game. But we will get to the after hour clubs in a little bit. When the track was over around 11pm and the afterhours places didn't open until after the bars closed 2:30 am, guess where we often ended up for 2-3 hours? A strip club! Most of the time we ended up at a club on 8 mile called Body Rock. The guys I came with were regulars there. To give you a little further insight, these guys bet, won and lost tens of thousands of dollars a night. It was pretty common for them to be carrying $30,000 to $50,000 each. You didn't leave that kind of money in your glove box , but you never knew what one might have in their trunk. Besides having large sums of money, most of these guys had no real respect for money. It came easy and spent freely. So when they went in to a club everyone from the valet car parker, to the coat check girl, to the doorman, to the waitress's and bartenders and especially the dancers were tipped well. The staff knew where their money came from and focused their attention on the source of the money. What was interesting about Body Rock is that it was sort of a mixed club. While I don't think it was discriminatory by design clubs in Detroit catered to certain crowds. They played urban music, had predominantly black dancers and catered to a crowd that enjoyed that. Other clubs stayed away from the urban music, played rock and roll and had mainly white dancers. Some bars were very upscale others were very blue collar working class locations. Reflecting back what made Body Rock interesting is that they had a pretty mixed crowd of customers and dancers. The guys I was with had a lot of money and were happy to spend it. There were many other people in the bar on a regular basis that also had plenty of money and also liked to spend it. In the late 70's early 80's money flowed in the streets in Detroit. The Casinos hadn't opened yet. Dope and dope money was everywhere and this filtered in to the clubs. In quoting a close friend of mine that used to DJ he often at the end of the night told the crowd "You don't have to go home, but you can't stay here". So the party often overflowed to the afterhours clubs where dancers wanted to continue drinking and powdering their noses and often dancer money ended up in the fruit machines. Of course customers of the dancers followed the dancers to the afterhours locations. It was an interesting co-dependent mixture, money attracted women to dancing and gorgeous women attracted men with money. In a classic economic model deals came together where men parted with money and women pleased men.

Although it was over 35 years ago, my first visit to a strip club is still vivid in my mind. It was a new world to me. I had never experienced anything like it. The sounds, sights and smells. The gathering of so many different variations of people customers, staff and dancers. I was fascinated and intrigued. The people interested my from a sociological and psychological perspective. The actual business and all the moving parts related to it made me think. The accessibility to me of physically exquisite women was mind boggling at a personal level. This chain of events took me into a world that some have visited and most men have fantasized about. This book is a story you will find entertaining. It is also a text book that will educate you with a real life foundation about the industry. It will give you insight into dancers, what makes them tick. You can explore this world vicariously through my words. Depending on your agenda and goals you will benefit from my experiences. As we move forward from the introduction to the real subject matter, please keep a few main concepts in mind. This is a ***business*** about ***fantasies.*** Always remember this the better the fantasy the better the business. Don't lose track of reality, it is a fantasy! In this business ***Dancers are the utmost of importance***, nothing else really matters and are only details. If you have dancers, happy dedicated dancers everything else will follow. If you're a customer, employee or potential owner of a club I hope you enjoy this book and learn from it.

# Thank You!

This book wouldn't be complete without some Thanks to many people. It would be impossible to list everyone. Years later, it's possible that many of you might not want to be listed. In fact I hesitated to write this book. Knowing that many people I know could have some negative feelings about me and my involvement in this industry made me wonder if it made sense. At the end of the day, I have no regrets. I always conducted myself ethically. Clearly the industry has some negative effects on some people. Conversely like many things in life it's what you make of it.

**Superfly**, thanks for bringing me into a club for the first time as well as so many of the things you have taught me in life. I enjoy our conversations and friendship to this day.

**Francis**, thanks for being a great friend and teaching me so much. Your unique personality and genuine balance of kindness for people balanced with business sense is one of a kind. Your personal expertise and knowledge of the industry is second to none.

**Michael**, Thanks for always being a friend. For being so gracious to me over the years in your clubs. Answering my questions and mentoring me.

**Victor, Jimmy, Pia, Sherie & Alex,** Your all assets to the clubs you associate with. Over the years I have enjoyed a personal friendship with all of you as well as being a customer. Each of you brings a unique set of skills and style and all of you have taught me a lot.

**Christine**, you were the 1st dancer I dated and what an experience it was.

**Tina,** I could write a book just about you. You became a very special part of my life and still are and always will be.

**Becky**, You're a great woman. I enjoy our friendship and someday would still like to finish counting your freckles.

**Bridgette**, you are a special soul, thanks for always being there.

**Sheila**, I count you as one of my best and closest friends. Although we are both in different places in our lives. Whenever I talk to or see you it's like time has stood still. Thank you for Cody and lets grab a piece of cheese cake.

**Nicole,** you are a great friend, business partner and a wonderful source of introductions.

**Ron**, EMR was a great venture. I appreciate the opportunity you created and all you taught me

**Scott,** It's always been interesting and good even when it was bad. Looking forward to the next project.

**Mark E,** I always enjoyed sitting with you, watching you operate, we had great fun.

**Roy,** you have been a good friend and partner in crime.

**Shawn,** You have been a great friend.

**Amanda** I could never forget you.

**Bob,** for a minute I thought you might end up being my brother in law. I always enjoy hanging out with you and look forward to projects of ours.

**Nikki** I hope all is good.

**Kelly,** I had to mention you, why were you always so difficult?

**Eva** It was always interesting.

**Carly** you are a diamond in the rough. I hope you find yourself and have a great life!

**Morgan** I don't know where to start and hope it never ends. You have taught me so much. I wish I could bring you into my head and you could see the world through my eyes. I wish you knew what I know. You are very loved and always will be!

**Cindy,** For a young girl I can't fathom the level of maturity and worldliness you have. You always made me happy to be around you.

Over the past 30 years I have had the pleasure to meet and interact with so many people. I couldn't mention all of you as it would take up a whole book. As this book develops many other people will be mentioned. People come and go. Some I have stayed in touch with others I have lost contact with. My experiences will always remain with me. So many people contributed to my experiences. These people are parking lot attendant and valet car parkers. The first people you see when you get to a club. The door people who check Id and take cover. The coat check people. Doormen that locate a place to sit. Waitresses and shot girls. Of course the entertainers. DJ's. Bathroom attendants. Finally all kinds of people that shared my experiences. People who I met via the clubs. People I would say hi to and that would great me. I might not ever know their names. Others were friends of the staff. Many were people like me that enjoyed the atmosphere of a club. As I'm writing this I'm thinking of so many people that I haven't mentioned that I should. Please know and recognize that I appreciate your friendship.

# Glossary

**Agent** – or Agency. A person or organization that recruits and provides dancers to the clubs. Often this function is in house

**Assistant Manager** – Second in command during a shift. Assists the manager in running the club.

**Bar Back** – Assistant to the Bartenders, stocks coolers, gets ice, washes glasses…

**Bartender** – Takes care of the drinks and the beverage component of the bar.

**Bouncer** – Typically a big guy that extinguishes problems and if someone needs to be asked to leave facilitates this.

**Cover** – The amount of money charged for admission.

**Dance Card** – Also called a permit. Many Governmental entities regulate Dancers and employees and require a license/card/permit to be able to legally work in a club.

**DJ** – Disk Jockey. Now most music is on hard drives but the name stuck. They are tasked with running the show, announcing the girls, selecting the music, setting the rotation of the dancers…

**Doorman** – could also be a bouncer. They stand at the door, check ID, greet customers, find them a seat, often take cover…

**Dressing Room** – Where the performers dress and undress. A place away from customers.

**House Mom** – She manages the dressing room, helps the girls with costumes, hair… Makes sure there is nothing unusual going on in the dressing room. Often provides snacks, cosmetics…

**Lights** – Lots of lights in a strip bar. From the outside of the club to the stage. They always need work and improvement.

**Manager** – Runs the club for the owners and might also be an owner. Schedules the help, Hires and fires people. Orders Liquor. Handles the money in the club. Opens and closes. Is an ambassador to customers. Often does accounting in reporting daily figures to owners.

**Permit** – See Dance Card. Also could refer to various licenses required for a club to operate.

**Regular** – a customer that is regularly at the club.

**Rotation** – The order that dancers go on stage(s) .

**Set** – The number of songs a dancer might do on stage.

**Shot Girl** – There is a trend in clubs where a girl goes around with a tray of shots and asks patrons to buy shots. Shots are small portions of a drink.

**Sound** – The sound system, the music selected and played…

**Stage** – What  it sounds like the area where the performers perform. Often there is multiple stages in a club.

**Tip Out** – is concept where dancers "Tip Out" give or share tips with the other employees of a club. Often the house mom, the DJ  and the doormen/bouncers. Beyond that most clubs have gone to a model where the dancers do not get paid by the club, they are deemed to be independent contractors  and actually pay the club to work there. So they Tip Out to the club a fee to work.

**Valet** – The guys that park the cars and bring them around to you. Often they provide other services. They will go fill up your car, get it detailed…Others just park and bring you your car.

**VIP Room** – This is the newest craze in Men's clubs. Often it's not a room but an area like a closet with a bench and a curtain. The idea is that patrons can select a dancer and take her to a private area (VIP ) area where she can perform for him. The level of performance can go to extremes. Clubs have found this as a great source of revenue charging the patrons and dancers additional money to use these areas. The regulatory agencies hate these VIP areas as they assume much more is going on than dancing and often there is.

**VJ** – Video Jockey usually the same as the DJ, but is in charge of what is displayed on the clubs video screens. This includes Sporting events and music videos. Promotional videos of the club and future events…

**Waitress** – the person that serves you your drinks and food.

# Overview

This book will appeal to many readers. Some of you are looking for entertainment. Reading entertainment. Others are thinking about wanting to open or invest in a club and want to learn more. Some of you are intrigued by the industry and want to get a better understanding of how it works. Many of you love beautiful strippers and want to get a real perspective of what drives them. What the think. What makes them tick. And from your perspective and most relevant how do you get involved with them. Involved means different things to different people. Most of you want sex. Others are enamored with the idea of having a trophy stripper as the other half of your relationship. Beyond that Strippers are real people with great personal qualities and make wonderful girlfriends and wife's. But there is dynamic to them that needs to be understood if you're going to get involved with them. Many parts of this book will be simplistic to many of you. Please keep in mind the book is written for everyone with interest. Like most things in life people experiences, knowledge and ability to learn is all over the place. What is simple to you is new to someone else. So let me take you under my wing and teach you what I know. I feel that as readers and purchasers of my book I also owe you the right to ask further questions. Please feel free to use the email address in the beginning of the book. I'm also available to consult on projects relating to the industry. Let's get started.

# The Blueprint of the club

Many of you will find this section irrelevant. Keep in mind that there are many types of people that will be reading this book and some of them may have never stepped foot into a club. Others may be thinking of opening a club and have interest in design. Let's start off with the basics of what every club should have and then work our way through the club. There are a few guiding principles when thinking about a club. It must be appealing to the staff and customers in design and function. It should maximize the use of the square footage with profit in mind. The design should work well with the business model. Let's start with the outside of the club. Most people coming there will know of it as their destination. While occasionally someone might be driving by and say "oh a strip club, let's check it out" most of the customers know where they are going. So from the outside, in my opinion it's best not to flaunt your business to antagonize local residents and religious organizations. There is no reason not to be a good neighbor, in fact it helps. You can have curb appeal and recognition without smut. Unfortunately much of this will be dictated by what your buying into. But if you have the luxury of starting from scratch, think all this through.

# Driveway and Parking

Lets start with the drive way and parking lot. 1$^{st}$ detail make sure you have good closed circuit TV  that is recorded off premise. This will protect you in many ways. It will provide a record of who came and went at what time. It will give you a basis to do some down and dirty accounting. Just as a simple example. 100 cars during a shift implies 100 or more patrons. This should give you 100 cover charges 250 drinks sold... If the lay out allows you I would have a separate employee parking area and entrance. All kinds of problems can occur at shift change and closing. Dancers and customers have been drinking. Often their agendas and plans aren't the same. If you can send them on their separate ways it avoids issues at your club. Try to designate a special area for people being dropped off or  waiting for a Cab, Uber, Limo, Party Bus. Back to the drive way, try to have some clear flow of traffic. Make it easy to understand where to pull into , how to leave etc. Your lot should be clean. It's common to find empty beer cans and bottles and assorted garbage daily. Stay on top of it. Garbage cans near the entrance make it easy for a patron to throw away whatever they need to prior to entering the club. Landscaping will be dictated by your climate. Use it to your advantage. Lighting is important. Your location should be well lit at night. Keep your lot up.

A big question comes up regarding valet parking. Do you offer it or not? There are advantages and disadvantages. Financially it can add to your bottom line but it can also be a problem. So much depends on your cliental. As a customer if I personally have a choice I don't like valet parking. I just don't want someone in my car. Conversely if I have to park very far away I'm like most people a little lazy. In climates where there is a cold winter, it's nice to get into a warm car that has had the snow removed. If you utilize valet parking, make sure you have quality CCTV that is recorded that you can go back to if a customer claims their car was damaged. Make sure you have views of both sides of the car and a head on shot and exit rear end shot. Over time the system will pay for its self over and over. Your Valets should be responsible for your exterior of the building. This includes keeping the lot clean, the garbage cans emptied and depending on the extent and size of your facility  the landscaping and snow removal. You can keep the Valet service in house, ie your employees. Or alternatively you can hire a valet service or enter into a rental agreement with them. The challenge is finding good reliable honest valets. If you decide to rent your lot, make sure you have a good contract that allows you to terminate it if you're not satisfied. Always have the proper insurance for valet parking and if required whatever permits. Keep your prices for valet within reason. No one wants to feel they got mugged prior to walking in the door. Make sure your valets are clean and friendly. I know of many clubs that utilize pretty girls as valets. The general rule is , how would you feel parking your car?

The other option is to offer patrons the ability to park their own cars. Some places still charge their patrons to park others don't. Often a clubs location dictates that some sort of guard should be watching the cars. Whomever has this responsibility should be in uniform so there is no question who they are and be friendly. The CCTV view of the lot can also be played in the club. You want patrons to feel comfortable and safe coming and leaving your club.

Employees in any variation should have a clear understanding where to park. If possible a separate employee entrance is best. If you can use the employees cars in a way that make your club look busier it can't hurt. You should have a procedure in place to make sure employees that shouldn't be driving get home. Depending on your location and the employee a Uber or cab is often a good choice. If you have Valet parking it's nice for the valets to clean off all the cars in the winter. Depending on the weather start the cars and turn on the ac or heat prior to close with the car owners permission.

It's always a good idea to have a set of jumper cables or a battery boost box handy. Car opening tools for a lock out also are needed more then you can imagine. A tank of compressed air for flats and low tires is also good to have. If it's easy a can of spare gas is suggested. Anticipate any issues a car might have. Your goal is to get these people safely off your property at closing and on their way. A preferred towing company that is responsive to you should be in your phones.

It's sounds simplistic but there should be a written set of rules and procedures on how your lot should be run. We all have heard first impressions are critical. The first impression a patron gets is driving onto your club and the person that greets them.

You should always empower and reward your valets to add to your marketing list. They should have a notebook and pen and ask customer if they are on the VIP list? Offer them patrons special invitations to VIP Invite only events... Of course make sure they understand that email and texts will be from the club.

As a patron coming into a club, I want it to be obvious what I should do. Where I should park... It's nice to be greeted in a friendly way. I also like to feel comfortable knowing my car is safe. Leaving the same principals applies. It's nice to have someone send you on your way with a cheerful good bye, see you soon, hope you had fun, thanks for coming by...From a price perspective it really doesn't matter. I have seen clubs with free parking to $20 parking. Like most people that go to a club, I'm not on a budget. But I don't want to feel like I have been mugged. Price points should be where it allows a patron to tip the valet a few dollars easily like $3 or $7. Thus the Valets often get a $5 bill or $10 bill.

# Lobby & Entrance

This is where the experience should start. It should be overwhelming and over the top. This is where most clubs fail. Every guest enters here, you have their attention and you have the ability to make an impression. Make it a great impression and make it count . I would urge you to hire the most attractive employee available for this position. She should be stunning, friendly and smart. This is a great position to hire for and graduate employees towards dancing. Many attractive girls have a stigma about dancing. They feel dancing is not for them, but being a hostess is in their wheel house. Like the parking lot and most areas of the club I'm a big advocate of Closed Circuit TV. There should be a view of the main doorway, who is coming and going. Your hostess should be checking id to make sure the people entering the club are of age. There are actually scanners that scan id and interface with the CCTV system so you never have an issue regarding under age patrons in your club. Some of these id scanners also capture name and address data to build your mailing list. Your hostess should collect cover charges, a recorded view of the cash register keeps everyone honest. If you have VIP cars that allow free admissions (and you should) I'd suggest these people sign in on a clip board and if your cash register system allows for it they be rung up with no monetary value but to keep a count. If your club is in a climate where people wear coats it's best to offer the ability for your patrons to check their coats. Most clubs make this mandatory from a security perspective. Keep your fee for coat check minimal and have a big tip jar. In fact I would suggest you don't charge for coat check, just let your guests tip your coat check attendant. You want to use this entrance way to promote future events and you should events on a regular basis. Have a prominent location for a poster or a TV screen that runs video commercials promoting the event. Your hostess should always be collecting email addresses and phone numbers to text people invitations and information for events. Patrons should also be invited to upcoming events by the hostess. AS patrons come in they should be asked " Will you be  joining us for _____insert event here (The fight, Football Game, Amateur Contest..) May I add your name to the VIP Guest List. Again this is a common fail in many clubs. You have a guest standing there in front of you, make this guest feel special and they will become a repeat revenue producing customer for life. If possible a window between the lobby and the parking valet where a customer can give their valet ticket to the parking people prior to going outside is desirable. Keep the temperature appropriate for the weather so people come into an  inviting atmosphere. Keep the lobby clean, provide a garbage can and if smoking is allowed in your club have a ash tray. The area should be inviting and welcoming. It should be a nice experience to walk in and orderly enter the club. You don't want to make a patron feel like they are being stuck up as the enter your club. It should be the opposite they should feel excited and happy.

As a patron, learn the names of the hostesses. Make sure you also great them as you enter and leave. At some point you may want to use them as a reference or introduction to a dancer.

It's always nice to have a new friend. No matter what your agenda is, the hostess can be an asset. She knows who's working, and who is not. She knows who came with who. This may seem not real relevant but it is. It's time for me to tell you one of my funny stories and an important lesson I learned a long time ago. I'm a creature of habit. It works for me. When I was hanging out in a club looking to date strippers I stuck to my habits. I took an old sales persons approach. Pitch enough potential people and someone should bite. Others use a more vernacular cruder expression, "If you throw enough shit against a wall some will stick". So at this time in my life I was single, fascinated with dancers and wanted one for myself. I had a routine that worked for me most of the time. It was sort of a sales funnel, fill it up with leads and keep it full and work what was coming out of the bottom. Early on it was evident to me that dancers get hit on all the time. In fact many of them feel and are empowered by this behavior of men throwing themselves at them. I didn't want to be considered a customer because this made the relationship professional , I would be paying to play. I wasn't bad looking but no one has ever accused me of being a movie star. I didn't use drugs. So I had to use my brains and personality to accomplish my goals. I didn't want to appear desperate. Many dancers have a rule not to date customers or people they meet at a their work. I wanted results but couldn't be sitting in the same bar every night. Dancers are in their own world. First most people have preconceived notions about them. Thus dancers have a hard time initiating a normal relationship as they feel most men see them as easy, slutty… or at best not relationship material. Conceptually who wants their woman getting naked for a bunch of other men? Dancers really have little respect for men that patronize clubs so I had to be different that typical normal and regular customers. As a practical matter dancers also keep some pretty unusual hours that oppose normal working people. They leave work late at night/early in the morning. (unless the work a day shift). Usually they just don't go home and go to sleep. So typically they are often going to sleep when most people start their work day. They are getting up when most people are starting to unwind after work. Their co – workers, other dancers, waitresses, bartenders, bouncers keep similar hours. It never struck me that dancers may be roommates, friends come to work together etc. So early on I was embarrassed but fortunately really wasn't real out of line when I pitched two different dancers that I didn't know were roommates. It was funny when they came out of the dressing room together both sat down with me and took me up on my plan as a team. Fortunately for me while not by design by me it worked out better than I could have ever planned. Thus the moral of this story is learn all you can.

# Please Come in

Clubs like dancers come in all shapes and sizes. They all serve their purpose and everyone has their preference. I want to start with a concept that many clubs do well and others fail at, the ambiance of the club. It should be comfortable and inviting. You should be able to use all of your senses. The lighting should allow you to see your surroundings. Subdued lighting hides stretch marks and other imperfections but you should be able to see. Sound systems should sound good, but you should be able to have a conversation. Most places do not allow smoking or allow it in special designated areas so tobacco smoke is less of a problem. Effects from smoke machines are nice in moderation. The temperature should be comfortable. And the club should be clean, especially the bathrooms. Common sense should prevail here.

# The Stage(s)

All clubs have a main stage, many clubs have multiple stages. The stage typically has a pole or multiple poles that the dancers do tricks on. Stages often are rectangular but also come in every shape. The design of the club should try to offer a good view of the main stage from all areas of the club. Thus the orientation and height of the stage is best designed to maximize the seating capacity of the club while maintaining visibility. Most stages have a tip rail, essentially a small ledge or counter deep enough for drinks that allow people to sit around the stage. This also makes it easy to accommodate wheel chairs. I have seen stages with extravagant architectural design and materials as well as very simple designs. If your building from scratch keep in mind that people really are looking at what's on the stage not at the stage. It's seldom a place to go over the top in cost and design. A great place to install sub woofers for the audio system is under the stage. Blowers with vents that can blow up a skirt like Marilyn Monroe's famous photo are a nice and inexpensive feature. Fog/smoke that fires from below the stage is also a nice effect. The surface of the stage needs to be able to be kept clean and take abuse and to be changed as needed. High density polyethylene is a great surface. Think of cutting boards. Neon and LED lights can be used to outline and highlight the stage. Good wide steps with hand rails are important for the dancers to get on and off the stage. If your design allows for it a fireman's pole that allows the dancers to enter the stage from a dressing room above is a great effect.     The same concepts apply to any side or satellite stages. If your club is large enough and the design works, the ability to rotate dancers among the stages is nice. Often the smaller stages cannot accommodate a tip rail. Try to place your satellite stage near something so you get additional utility out of it, like near your bathrooms, or VIP area , thus it keeps activity and excitement moving throughout the club.

# The Bar

The operant word when it comes to the actual Bar is functionality. This is the command and control center of your operation. The success and bottom line of your establishment assuming you have dancers and customers first is your ability to deliver drinks and service your patrons. While many people might disagree with me, I don't prefer to have customers sitting at the bar. We are not a sports bar or a shot and beer place. We are a gentleman's club While some customers prefer to sit at the bar, I as an owner prefer to have them sitting out on the floor at a booth, table, tip rail in the vip area…So I prefer a smaller bar over a larger bar given the choice. The less the customers can see of the inner workings behind the bar from my perspective the better. What I mean by this is the dirty glasses, the dish washer, the returnable beer bottles, the credit card machines… Show off liquor , beer, wine …I prefer a separate service area if possible for waitresses and shot girls. This area should be separate and easily accessible by them –v-elbowing away customers to order drinks. It also allows you to have a main bartender to service customers and a additional bartender to service waitresses. If your design allows for it a separate walk in cooler for your beer barrels, mixes and bottled beer storage (not behind the bar stock) is best. Be cognitive of what you sell, and stock it. Keep your beer delivery lines clean as well as your mixers. Stay on top of your $CO_2$ for your mixers. If possible have your ice machines behind the bar instead of bringing ice to the bar.

A nice display of what you carry is pretty easy attractively display. A tiered shelve system with LED lights adds a nice warmth to the bar, grouping like drinks together. I don't necessarily advocate carrying every flavor of every brand of Vodka as an example. But you should pick on brand an carry the full set of flavors. In time adjust to what you need. It's a common practice to price top shelf premium liquors very expensively. I know this is a losing strategy.  At a later point in this book we will discuss pricing strategies. For now just think along these lines. People have their favorite drink. Most people have a quasi budget of what they are going to spend and are aware of the cost of their favorite drink. As an owner we need to think about the whole operation from the profit margin of a drink to the income of our staff to the satisfaction of our patrons. Thus if we pour a 1.5 oz shot and a fifth contains 25.6 oz's we are getting 17 shots out of a fifth of liquor. Let's say a person drinks 4 drinks during a visit to our club.  Let's look at Jack Daniels #7 at $21.20 per fifth and Evan Williams at $12.69 per fifth. A difference of $8.51 per fifth or .50 per drink. (These are Michigan Wholesale prices at the time of the writing of this book) A person that drinks Jack and Coke wants Jack and Coke. If your charging $6 or more for this drink is it worth the .50 savings?  This isn't an easy question to answer. If you sell 100 Jack and cokes a day x 288 days a year (assuming your open 6 days a week) = 28,800 drinks. If you make an extra $2 per drink that is an extra $57,600 per year. Multiply that by 10 similar examples and you have an extra half a million dollars. But will you sell more drinks by offering them at a more palatable price? Hard to say. You know your clientele and market. People like some value and don't want to feel taken advantage of. Find a good middle ground. Always use fresh fruit, quality mixes… Put a good product in your customers hands.

POS systems. Not Piece of shit, point of sale. I strongly suggest them. At minimum they provide consistency. Whatever you set your drink prices at it charges properly. No more questions about when happy hour started, how much a certain drink costs…You will also glean information. What sells, what hours and days and you will be able to structure specials properly. From an inventory perspective it will simplify things. In every situation where you need data, it beats a z tape from the register. It will help you identify good servers and show you servers that may need some additional training. Data is good.

Beer. Like most people I thought more is better. In some ways it is. But as a practical matter you may only have so much room for storage. A good selection that will allow anyone to get something they like is the best strategy. Listen to your sales reps unless it's something new and then maybe try it. Carry a regular, lite, dark and few imports on tap. Make sure you have cold mugs and pitchers. Pitchers can be a problem or a blessing. Price them properly and you will be fine.

Shots are a new trend that can add a lot of revenue to the club but are also perceived negatively. No one wants to be bothered with " Do you want a shot? Would you like to buy the lady a shot?" If you are going to sell shots find the right talent to sell them. Shot girls are often great dancers in training.

Specials – great to have. Keep the customers and dancers happy. They add to total sales.

Wine – This gets interesting. Of course you should have a basic stock of a white wine and a red wine. I have seen some clubs do very well with a nice wine selection. I think this is very dependent upon your club, your customers and your food. Be open minded here and try different things. The same goes for Champagne. Stock a variety in both quality and price points. Champagne is fun. People perceive it as luxurious and relate it to celebrations and special times, keep that thought going. Small bottles known as splits are well received by dancers and have a great profit margin. Additionally dancers can drink many of them and not get as drunk compared to mixed drinks.

Soft drinks – not everyone drinks alcohol. Make sure you have fresh coffee and a good selection of soft drinks. There currently is a trend of people drinking energy drinks. See what sells and stock it.

The bottom line is have a good selection of drinks. Keep your price points where you have a margin but people don't feel they are being gouged. Pay attention to your glasses, napkins, stirrers , fruit…Put out a quality product.

# Food

Human beings need to eat. People get hungry. There is no reason not to offer food at a club. Some of the best food I have ever had has been at a club. Besides the atmosphere the food is genuinely great. As a club owner, food really can add to your bottom line in many ways. There is a nice margin and mark up in food. You will also see that the average stay of a patron is longer when you offer food and with that longer stay more money is spent. Your dancers not only have a chance to eat, but they will forge relationships with customers where the customers come in for a "date", they will have a meal, a drink or two and then often a trip to the VIP. All of these activities add to your bottom line.  While it's probably best to have your own kitchen and cook, don't let the lack of a kitchen stop you. There are a few options. The bet is to pick a restaurant close by and cut a deal with them. Create a menu based upon their menu, negotiate a deal that makes financial sense and create your menu. Alternatively find a sandwich shop that makes good cold sub's and go buy some. Get a case of chips. Put up table tents, a sub , chips and a drink for $10-$15. Or just offer the subs and chips. If you don't sell all the subs and it's time to get rid of them, send them home with the staff, they won't go to waste. If you do have your own kitchen there are many ways to structure the cost of the kitchen, try to avoid a salary or hourly pay for the cook. Make them your partner in the food. It will lead to a better product and more profit. Give them the responsibility of ordering and buying the food. Getting and keeping up the proper permits. You bring to the equation, customers, a facility, equipment, waitresses … For the right person it is a win - win situation. Conversely if the situation justifies it  hire a cook, give them a salary and delegate the related food tasks to them.

Food draws. A free buffet on Monday nights put out at the start of the Monday Night Football game during football season is a great way to pack your bar on what might be a slow Monday night. Some chicken wings, meatballs, cheese sticks, a vegetable tray, Cheese and crackers … is pretty inexpensive and will give you a nice return in your cash register. If you don't have a kitchen, order in a party sub, stop at a chicken place and get some wings and order in some Pizza it will work. Keep a well stocked vending machine. You never want a customer to leave because they feel like a snack.

# Booths, Tables...

Dependent upon the size of your club and your cliental you have many options. I suggest all of the options if you have the room. We spoke earlier on the concept of having a smaller bar to sit at to keep people on the main floor. Most of your customers will come alone or with a friend. On occasion you will get 4 people out together. If you market to it, you will get bachelor parties, softball teams and larger groups. Try to design your space where it is flexible. If you have a large party, design it where you can rope it off, put together some tables and make everyone happy. Booths are great, they allow for customer to have a little more privacy, to feel special, to grab a meal…How booths are reserved and utilized is an area of contention. Typically you ask the doorman for a booth and it's expected to tip the doorman. Over the course of the year as a club owner you are losing a ton of money to your doormen. I'd suggest that if you charge an extra fee, it goes on the customer tab, collected by the waitress and into your register. This also helps avoid a problem where a customer gets up to go to a vip area and is there for a while and the doormen seat someone else. The waitress should be more in touch with her section, knowing what I going on. Your tables should be quality. It sounds simple but you don't want a wobbly table. The size of the tables should be small enough to maximize your capacity, while being large enough for your customers to be comfortable. Make sure you have enough room between the tables for people to get up and around and for your staff to serve people. High tops are fine with stools in some areas. All chairs and the booths should be comfortable. You want people to sit and stay. They should also be easily cleaned. I'd also suggest a table tent on each table that gives people something to look at while promoting your club, drink specials, food specials and upcoming events. When designating sections to your waitresses the normal thoughts are to divide the club in sections like the front and the back. I'd prefer to give servers if they are capable of handling it tables all over. It keeps it interesting for the patrons and tends to make more money for the servers in tips. Keep the club well laid out. Have good lines of site to the stage(s). Make sure the staff can service all of the seating. Keep the seating comfortable. By doing all this you will keep people coming back.

# The Dressing Room

I want to start by saying the dressing room should be an area to change, to freshen up, NOT a place for dancers to congregate. Dancers in the dressing room don't make money, for themselves or for the club owner(s). Keep this in mind. Your dressing room should be large enough to accommodate your dancers and maybe other members of your staff. You should offer lockers so people can lock up their stuff. If size permits permanent assigned lockers are great. It has an element of retention to the dancers and makes it easier for them to come to work, knowing they don't need to drag certain items back and forth. You should have good electrical circuits with GFE plugs in the dressing room as there will be constant hair dryers, curling and straightening irons always plugged in. Good lighting and mirrors are a must. I prefer a no drinks in the dressing room policy, but often a dancer likes to have a drink while getting ready. If you allow drinks, make sure you have a bus station for empty glasses. Plenty of garbage cans are also helpful. A long bench in front of the counters and mirrors is preferable to chairs, no having to straighten it out, room for everyone and it discourages sitting for long periods of time. If there is room have enough space where you can have a hair stylist , a manicurist and a makeup artist come in. It costs you nothing, the girls pay them and will add to the exclusiveness of the club for the dancers and they will look better. Schedule these people on different slow days.

Bathrooms in the dressing room are a luxury of the use of space. You will always need a bathroom for female customers, but if your space allows it's a nice touch. I have seen showers in clubs but they are rarely used.

I'd suggest a locked showcase where you can post memos, schedules… for the girls to read. Especially upcoming events.

House mothers – I could go either way on this. The real problem is who pays them and how much. I hate having dancers having to tip the doormen, the dj, the house mother, the parking lot guy, pay tip out…You need an accountant and at the end of a shift it gets weird, the dj telling girls don't forget to see so and so. So if you have enough girl it's best in my opinion to pay the house mother directly from the bar. If the girls tip her so be it. What the house mother do is keep order in the dressing room. Less BS about she took my shoes, I'm missing money… Less problems in the dressing room with girls arguing about anything. I would suggest an intercom or phone system extension where the DJ can call the house mom rather than announcing it over the Sound system if someone doesn't show up on stage. Again keep the dressing room clean and comfortable.

# The DJ Booth

Lets talk about the DJ for a moment. I'm not going to make a lot of friends with this section and it's written not to disrespect anyone. DJ's should work for the club. They should be paid a salary and given a drink and or meal and that is it. If a dancer wants to tip them that is their choice not a requirement. I have seen more girls chased away by a DJ that wouldn't skip them, play their music... because the DJ didn't like their tip. A good DJ can make a club. They are the Master of Ceremonies, they keep the show running and entertain the crowd. They welcome customers. They announce specials and upcoming events. Important people DJ's are but not more important than the club and it's bottom line. Every major town has a school for broadcasting. I have never called one and said I needed a DJ and didn't get all I wanted

Your DJ should be tasked with handling the show. This means that part of their shift starts before the play their first song. They should know who is scheduled to work and who is there. If by some chance there appears to be a shortage of dancers they should let the manager know. They should set the order of dancers for their shift. Who goes first... insuring variety for the customers. In todays social media crazed world the DJ should update the clubs social media outlets with who is working, and any specials and up-coming events. A quick conversation with the manager about any drink specials and a stop in to the kitchen or a call to ask about the days specials. Touch base with the girls, ask if there is any new music they want added to their sets. The DJ should be aware of local sports, announcing the scores in progress. Often a drink special tied to the home team scoring works well. Any issues related to the clubs sound and lights should be mentioned or even better written up for the club manager. If there is a fog/smoke machine it should be filled. In close proximity to the DJ it's good to have a computer with a camera, where dancers can be asked to update their club pages or create one. Tweet that they are there. Make a post on facebook... Promotion is critical.

The atmosphere of the club starts with the owner and is executed by the management and the staff. Music and videos should be aligned with the plan. There should be well thought out plans and procedures on how to handle visits from fire inspectors, police and VIP guests. Speaking of VIP, there should be a simple process that the DJ knows to skip a dancer in a vip area with a guest. The DJ need to keep the show running smoothly and professionally .

# Men's Bathroom

Keep it clean. Eliminate graffiti. If it fits your club an attendant and shoeshine guy are nice to have. The more amenities and comforts the better.

# The VIP Area

As I'm writing this my heart is beating a little faster. This concept and discussion is so unique. What man wouldn't want to be alone with a beautiful woman that is prepared to entertain him? When you ask anyone what is the VIP area, it's described as a more private area and the promise or chance of a sexual encounter is always there. Going back to my old days, when I was pretty mischievous a dancer would approach me when I was a customer and ask me if I wanted a dance. If interested I'd say sure and I would be told a regular table dance is $10 and upstairs in the VIP area dances are $25. I'd ask what is the difference and I'd be told upstairs is more private, we can get more comfortable... At that point I usually said what the hell, give me one of each so I know the difference. We started with a regular dance and often I said that was fine and never took it further. Fast forward to today. I can't speak of every market but I'm familiar with most. In some markets like Las Vegas there really is no need for the girls to do anything more than dance. Sure there are exceptions. A know or hand often brushes against a customer. Plans are made for a carry out or after work activities but in the club it's pretty tame. Detroit is a different market many of the clubs are outright brothels. One discusses what they want a price is agreed upon and the dancer and customer go to a private area and these people do what they want in privacy and in violation of many laws. I'm not going to discuss the ethics or morality of this. It's a personal decision for the people involved. Much more to follow on this later.

So as we discuss the layout and design of the VIP area's again it really is dependent on your club and budget. I have seen space that is about the size of a small closet five feet wide by 4 feet deep with a little bench and a curtain in the doorway. I have seen slightly larger areas with more plush couches, a table for a drink a hook for the dancers outfit and a curtain or door. One of the nicest VIP areas I have ever seen is in the Hustler Club in Linclon Park, MI. There are a variety of rooms. Most have an upholstered bench, a flat screen TV, Volume controls for the sound, dimmers for the lights, a table for drinks and some have bathrooms. All are themed differently with associated paint, art...What is the common denominator in all the clubs is that this area is private and there is a cost associated to use it. Knowing what goes on in the VIP area, you want to design this area so it is productive for you. It's best to keep it away from the main entrances, sort of out of site and far enough away that if your club gets raided you have a fighting chance to make sure you have no issues in the vip area. I don't like curtains, they are used as napkins and towels, hard to keep clean. Curtains are inexpensive and offer some privacy while still having some sense of legitimacy but I would suggest a real door without a lock. The seating area should be vinyl so it can be cleaned easily. Eventually it will need to be replaced but that is a good thing, if it got worn out you made money. A waste basket is a must, some feel that it's a bad idea as there is potential evidence of prohibited activities in the wastebaskets. Hooks for costumes ... The size should be comfortable . I would suggest no carpeting something like tile is easier to keep clean. Sound from the sound system should be muted enough where people can have a conversation but dancers can still hear if they are being called. Lighting should be subdued but you should be able to see. If possible I like a dimmer for the lights and a volume control for the sound system. You want a understanding, diplomatic bouncer assigned to the VIP area. You should defiantly charge for use of this area. I'd suggest a onetime daily charge to the dancers and any customer that wants to use the area. I would suggest a wrist band that is sold. I prefer not to use the bouncer to sell wristbands, to much temptation. Whomever is selling the wristbands should be on CCTV. I have also seen yearly VIP cards sold that offer free admission to the club as well as the VIP area. The Bouncer in the VIP area should be aware of who is in the VIP area and communicate with the DJ to skip that dancer if they are called and in rotation. It's best to have an ATM machine near the VIP area. It promote the use of the VIP area. I have seen ATM's dispense U.S, Currency and Club Script. The advantage of this is that the money somewhat stays in the club thus the first say $40 of any withdrawal is in club script and can be spent anywhere in the club. Proximity to a bathroom for the men is great, often they need to clean up a little.

So keep your VIP area in line with the rest of your club. It should be functional, clean and safe. I have seen many places where city's have come down hard on clubs for having VIP rooms. One way around this problem that I have seen work very well is private conference rooms. One could have a business meeting. The room should contain a small conference table, chairs, a white board with markers. Some legal pads and pens. A phone, fax machine and computer. A small love seat... You get the idea. If a patron wants to have a business meeting with a dancer...Same principals apply as before but charge more.

We have taken a tour of a club. Looked at all of the various elements that make up a club. What is important is they experience and expectations. Customers really come to a club to interact with girls. Every other aspect of a club is available elsewhere . There is no shortage of good sports bars, fine restaurants or places to go hang out. What distinguished a men's club from the other places is women. Every club is a little different. The type of dancers and the experience that is offered goes to extremes of the spectrum. Later on in this book we will delve into dancers and every aspect of them. Knowing that dancers are the most important element of the club, all of the other pieces need to fit around them. Looking at the real world outside of the fantasy and experience of a club. Women come in all shapes and sizes. The differ in their level of education and experience. Their social economic make up and status is all over the place. Your club should be geared around the dancers you hire and the cliental that will come to see them. Everyone should be happy and comfortable.

**Pro shop -** If you have the area often in combination with the coat check or cover area it's nice to offer branded clothes from your club. Nothing gaudy, it needs to be worn out in public. There are tons of vendors that offer hats, polo or T shirts... Bumper stickers are nice and offer some great options for promotions.

# The Rest of the Staff

**Bartenders** – Should always be women. It just adds to the experience of the club. Your bartender(s) should have a blend of the following qualities. First they need to have a presence , both physical and intellectual. They should be attractive in the sense of the experience that a customer at a strip club is expecting. Attractive is subjective especially today. I would try to stay in the middle of the perception of attractive not going to any extreme. From a personality perspective they must be friendly and tolerant. They will be dealing with your staff and customers. They must be able to remember names and faces. They need to be friendly. They also need to be firm in dealing with the wait staff. They need to be honest. My policy has always been if any member of my staff wants to buy a customer a drink that is fine. We have a house tab and a notebook that goes along with it, just say who it was for and why. If it gets out of hand they lose that privilege. The bartender needs to keep the bar stocked. If anything is running low they need to ask the manager for it. The bartender need to stay on top of the fruit, olives, mixes, stirrers, napkins, glasses, syrup, draft beer … Drink specials need to be worked on by the bartenders, wait staff and manager and announced by the DJ. Schedules must be kept and requested changes conveyed to and approved by a manager. All drawers need to be counted before and after every shift. Credit card machines and POS systems used as directed. Keep the drinks flowing, the cash register full and the customers happy!

**Waitresses** – Need to take full responsibility for their sections. They need to be clean. The people sitting in their section need to be happy. There is a fine line between being a bug and being attentative to a table. They should always ask if the table wants any drink special. Food orders should be confirmed and brought out with the necessary extras such as ketchup, napkins… As food is consumed tables should be cleaned off with a joint effort of the buss staff. If a customer goes to the VIP keep the table for the customer. Unless he customer is known the customer should be offered membership in the clubs VIP club(s) and their information if they want to give it should be taken. Always introduce a new customer to the manager. Offer last call. Never rush a customer. Waitresses should look good and carry on a conversation with their customers to the extent that a patron wants to talk to them.

**Shot Girls** – If you use them they should be attractive and not be a bug.

**Bus Staff** – are assistants to the Bartenders, Waitresses and Kitchen as well as the whole club. I prefer clean cut non extreme looking people. It should be communicated to them what their responsibilities are. They should be on your clubs pay roll with no expectations of being tipped by the staff but if they are it's a bonus. Garbage should be emptied. Empties should go to the proper area. Cooler should be stocked or product brought to them from the storage area. Tables should be watched and empty glasses and plates… should be picked up. Dependent on the set up dishes and glasses should be washed and put away. When asked if busy hey should assist waitresses by bringing out food from the kitchen. Tables and chairs should be wiped down . If there is no bathroom attendant. They should maintain the bathroom making sure it's clean, has toilet paper, soap… The dancers bathroom needs to be handled with diplomacy. Any maintenance issues should be referred to a manager. Depending on how the bar is cleaned often the bus staff will also clean after the bar closes. I always like to clean at the end of the day. It keep the fruit flies down, the bar smelling cleaner…

**Bouncers/Doormen** – Critical to your success. They can be a liability or a great asset. Violence never is productive but sometimes can't be avoided. You need and want people that can handle themselves but also prefer to be diplomatic. I would suggest you have them dress in black pants and white tuxedo shirt. We will get to how others dress later. Again I would make them employees of the club, pay them by the hour or shift. Tips are a bonus not an expectation. You should have a clear policy and job description for them. In time you will find the right people. The right person can double as a manager. Time for a quick story. On evening I was in my club and some guy came in and started spitting on a dancer on the stage. Swearing at her saying nasty things… Common thought process is to grab him and show him the door. I decided to talk to him. I went over to him and said come sit down at the bar. He did. Had he not it would have been different. I bought him a drink, while my bus boy quickly cleaned up the stage. I asked him what was going on and what would he do if he was me. He immediately became very apologetic. It was his girlfriend on stage and for whatever reason he was mad at her. I explained to him that we can't just have people coming in here swearing and spitting. He apologized again and whatever issues he had never came back to the club. Always best to be diplomatic, but protect your club.

**Manager and Assistant Manager** – Really important people. It's best to have someone with experience but hard to find. You can find managers from other types of bars but a good manager of a strip club isn't usually looking for a job so you need to develop them. Again I prefer women, it adds to the whole experience. There are plenty of talented women out there. The most important aspect of this job is to execute the vision and plan of the owners. Your manager is your General, your Chief of Staff they do it all. You can't micro manage them as you have delegated the running of your club to them. They are responsible for all areas of the club. Typically you have one General manager and a few assistant managers. I insist on a weekly meeting where all are present with the owner. Often there are phone calls among the staff. All of them are responsible for hiring and firing staff. Typically if there is a dispute about letting someone go the person that wants to retain that person keeps them exclusively on their shift. Applications are taken for employees during all shifts. The GM usually makes the schedule with everyone's requests in mind. The idea is to accommodate everyone. It rarely works perfectly and changes happen but you need to start somewhere. The assistant managers report to the GM on any matter relating to maintenance and ordering of product. The GM typically orders product and manages the maintenance contractors. The GM oversees the cash in the club, making sure that the registers are cleared out at the end of shifts, that sales are properly recorded as directed by the owner. Sales include all revenue (VIP Rooms, Cover, Coat Check, Parking, Vending Machines, Food…) Banking is done as directed keeping a certain amount of cash for operation and change and the rest given to the owners or deposited. Payroll is called in typically to a payroll company and checks are distributed on pay days, often cashed by the bar. The GM and Assistant should circulate during operational hours and meet and greet customers and interface with the staff keeping them focused. The club should be opened and closed by the manager at appropriate times. One of the managers needs to be there to receive product. Drink and food specials should be called by the manager. Basic analysis and forecasting should be done by the GM with the intent of always improving the business. Any issues should be written up and forwarded to the owners. I could write a full HR description here but is it beyond the scope of this book. Essentially the GM with their assistant runs the club.

**Coat Check Girl** – If your climate supports the need to wearing coats, you probably want to have a coat check and coat check girl. She should be attractive and like to talk. I prefer to offer free coat check and have a big tip jar. Have the girl work for tips. If not keep the price reasonable. Always have a flyer with the upcoming events available at the coat check as people leave. This person should also sign up people for the clubs VIP list and be compensated for this.

Lets talk about **uniforms**. They serve a purpose, they distinguish who is an employee in the club. They dress up the club. They add consistency to the experience. They also are an expense and hassle. I find it easier to dress everyone in white shirts and black skirts or pants. If you want uniforms there are all kinds of choices. I suggest the staff dress up on themed events. Local team jerseys for game night…The staff should always look nice and kempt. Your managers and assistant managers need to look and should look professional . Men should wear a suit and tie or a sports coat and turtleneck. Women should wear a business suit or something provocative but professional looking. Bus Boys are fine in jeans and a white t shirt or club shirt. DJ's are not seen and can dress as they want. Unless you have a wireless microphone and they get out among the crowd and then black pants and white dress shirt. Your valets should dress nicely and it should be clear who they are with a club hat or shirt or jacket. Your people should look professional and be a good representation of the club. This also will lead to better attitudes more professionalism and a better experience for everyone.

# Dancers

This is the center of attraction, the reason for the existence of the club. The product and service that brings the customers. In this section we will discuss dancers and employees of a club. Later on we will focus on them in other contexts. The biggest mistake club owners and their staff make is not recognizing the importance of dancers and the impact they have on the clubs success and bottom line. So often they are treated as a commodity prior to a club reaching critical mass and market penetration. Once you have 50+ dancers a night, $250,000 a week in sales and a mature staff you can start being tough and selective on your dancers. Until then it's critical to recruit and keep them happy.

Let's discuss the psychology of your customers. They are coming to your club for the dancers. There are many reasons they come for the dancers. Often it's a thing to do, boys night out, have some drinks and look at naked women. For others it's the pursuit of sex. Some people are bored and need to talk to a woman. Others are out right perverts with sex addiction problems. Others overlap all or some of these groups. The common denominator is they are coming for the dancers. There are many other places they can go out to drink and usually much less costly. If they are hungry they have all kinds of choices for food. If it's exclusively sex they are looking for they can call an escort . Knowing that they can go to a location that is safe, spend a little money and have access to naked women that want to talk to them (of course for money) is a big draw. Dancers dance for many reasons but their bottom line is money. Most people (dancers) don't want to stand on their feet for 6-8 hours in high heels, always being perky and friendly, speaking to strange men ( strange and unknown to them) and being propositioned, asked for their number and sex for hours at a time. For the girls who do extra's it's a mean to an end. A way to get the money they want and need in a way that works for them. So you have a match here. A model that works.

For this to model to work you need to have customers and dancers at the same time. Customers want to walk into a bar with a variety of dancers. If there is a shortage of dancers the customers experience is flawed. They don't have a variety to chose from. If they see something they like it's often rushed, the girl needs to attend to other customers or get on stage. For Dancers many of the same principals apply. They want to work where there is customers. They don't want to go into work and not make money. So it's a chicken and hen thing, which comes first? As an owner you actually control both sides of the equation but it's the dancers we are talking about. They are harder then customers. Do what you can and need to so that you keep them. If you have dancers, customers will com, stay and come back.

When I started my first bar I recognized this issue. While there was a lot of buzz and hype about the "New Bar" and I knew tons of dancers, converting this buzz and relationships into a successful club and a strong bottom line was an effort. Especially in the competitive market I was in. So I had to dig deeply into my phone book and my mind and apply everything I knew on how to make this work. I devised a pretty easy solution. I would call friends and people I know that enjoyed topples bars and asked them to help me. I would tell them come to the bar, I want to give you $100 to get some dances with, I need to make the place start happening. This worked. My associates came in and bought some drinks. They spent the money I gave them on dances. The dancers made some money that they paid me in tip out money. It really didn't cost me anything but I didn't make much either. But there was activity. When people walked in there were dancers. Dancers had some good days and slow days but They always made their tip out. My friends were happy and eventually momentum took over. I was pretty hands on. I couldn't really afford a manager and I wanted to make sure my project went the way I designed it. By design and as a practical matter Finding and keeping dancer was my mission.

So when recruiting dancers they typically fall into two categories, brand new and experienced. I'll start with brand new. It's best to advertise in college news papers, online and go out in person. Online works well and it's free. College news papers are ok, the challenge is typically the geographic distance between the college and the club, but the good news is college coeds usually come in quantity. Recruiting in person works best. I would typically take a few dancers out with me at night to a dance club, the dancers would talk to any pretty girl they could find. They would tell them they dance well, they are pretty… What do they do for a living? Would they be interested in making a thousand + dollars a week? They tell them about the club and then bring them over to me and introduce them. I would buy them a drink, pitch them on working give them a card, ask them for their contact information and invite them to the club. It's a never ending process but over time it works.

As for the experienced dancers they are a whole different breed. You have to assume there are some issues if they are coming to a new club. This is because if they are good they should be doing fine where they are. Dancers get in trouble. They don't keep a schedule. They use drugs and or get drunk. They argue with other dancers and the staff and eventually they are told to leave. Rarely did a dancer with experience show up and be issue free. Some of the benefits of experienced dancers is that they come with customers and are friends with other dancers. So you need to speak with them and see what their story is or let them tell it to you. I was just honest with them. I told them that I needed them. Sometimes it's just a little accommodation that they need. Flexibility in schedule…But you can't build a business on exceptions especially a business some human / dancer dependent. But do the best you can in hiring attractive dancers that fit your clubs needs. And always be upgrading.

In hiring dancers you need to understand your club and its clients. This goes back to your basic plan. Are you a club that caters to a younger hip hop crowd? Or older hippies that like classic rock and roll? Or perhaps a well to do cliental of business men and yuppies? You can't be everything to everyone and it doesn't work. So you pick your direction, play the music that is consistent with that direction and hire your dancers accordingly. The mainstream thought process is to hire young hard bodies, 10's and make few exceptions. This works to the extent that you can find and hire them but it isn't sustainable. First of all there is a limited supply of these types, Secondly if you club isn't hopping they can and will go work where the money is. Often you will find one that would rather work smarter at your club with less competition and being the star of the show. There is someone for everyone. Some men like their women "Short and thick" Others prefer red heads. For some only blondes and it goes on and on. So it's beneficial to have a variety of dancers. It's not my position to tell you who not to hire. There is a famous saying "Beauty is in the eye of the beholder". I have seen some really rough looking dancers out there. What you will find is young pretty girls have friends that are also young and pretty. Nothing racist here but women of certain ethnicity typically have friend of similar ethnicity. And rough worn out dancers often have similar friends. While these women tend to show up and work because they have limited choices of where to work. You don't want to be the last stop in your area for the end of dancers careers. Don't be apprehensive about hiring lot's of girl next door types. Hire a variety of ethnic girls. An older woman or two is good for the older guys and sets a good example for the younger girls. The process tends to work itself out, just don't get in the vicious cycle of hiring anything that walks in the door because you need girls it's a ;losing strategy.

At some point you will be approached by an agent or multiple agents. Like any profession there are good and bad agents. I would avoid them, you can do anything they can and more, you own the club, they are selling a position. Stay out of the competitions clubs at least not to poach girls. It's bad business and really doesn't go well. Just do your job, run your adds, hit the regular clubs and it will happen. Also speak to your regulars and your dancers. Ask them who they know and reward them for bringing their friends. It's pretty easy to offer any dancer free tip out any night she brings a new friend with her. Amateur contests can be fun if you get enough participants

So let's move forward in this process. You have a response to your recruiting. You have dancers showing up. Your next step is to keep them. They are there for the money, understand that. You know as well as they do when there is a slow day. There is no reason to beat them up over tip out. If they didn't make a little money it goes a long way to take them aside individually, tell them you recognize it was slow. Tell them not to tell anyone else, but you appreciate them and what they add to the club and let them know that today you will cover their tip out and tomorrow should be better. This is a worst case scenario. You have a business to run, be professional. Whomever is in charge of collecting tip out should be systematic and consistent. Often this function is delegated to the DJ, they are sitting in the same spot all shift, they have a list of the dancers and it just makes things efficient. As it gets towards the end of a shift I prefer to have a manager finish up collecting the money. It works best.

So let's get into the heads of our dancers. I'm talking psychologically not literally. Actually let's talk a little about getting involved with our dancers as co-workers. First it happens. Second it usually is problematic. When you have a somewhat secluded environment like a club, it becomes a society or community within itself. The nature of the industry, the hours of operation and all of the other moving parts just make it natural for people to interact with each other and get involved. As a owner or manager, employees look at you as an authority figure. In fact you are. You control the keys to their kingdom. You are powerful, you have money. You have the mechanism that generates money. You can do them favors, give them the best shifts, let them slide on tip out, be flexible if they want to come in late or leave early. Buy them drinks and the list goes on and on. Further if you own a club or manage one, well not always it typically implies that you have some natural intelligence, common sense, business sense, people skills… and this is attractive. Owning a club or managing one doesn't typically work well with a Main stream orthodox family life. It takes a very secure significant other (Wife, Fiancé or Girlfriend) to not question what their spouse is or isn't doing at work. It's hard not to come home with out smelling like perfume and to have some makeup on you. The hours you keep in operating a club just don't work well with a typical family life. You would usually get home in the early hours of the morning and sleep through the early part of the day. Most clubs are open 7 days. Thus if you're a good owner or manager, you are on top of your investment and or job. You are at your club, not home. There is also a perceived negative social stigma associated with the industry. Imaging your kids in school when asked what does their parents do saying my daddy owns a strip club. Conversely all of the previous mentioned considerations have little effect on a stripper, waitress or bartender being involved with a club owner or manager. They are in the business. They understand it. On a daily basis they live the business . This makes it easy and in fact encourages relationships. Often the power of a club owner or manager goes to their head. This happens in degrees. It's easy to get a swollen ego when you have beautiful women throwing themselves at you on a regular basis. Where the problem occurs is that a natural function of this relationship builds jealousy among the rest of the staff. " She gets special treatment because she's f-cking the owner/manager". Probably correct and goes with the territory. Thus if you get involved with an employee, and this advice is in general not just the strip club industry, use your head (the one on top of your shoulders) think through how others perceive your relationship and how you treat your significant other. Know that if it doesn't work out, typically you will also lose an employee. On the other hand it goes a long way in being close to your help. It builds a team, it build loyalty and it builds cash in your registers and this cash flows to you. From my experiences, most dancers have some exit plan in their head, to quit dancing, settle down etc. Their timing usually is off to settle down and they are working. There is nothing wrong with asking a person about their aspirations and future. If it's true there is nothing wrong with sharing in their vision. It is a losing strategy to be dishonest, lead someone on and this never ends well.

When I was younger, prior to ever stepping foot into a strip club I would often go out on a date and end up in a little city in Michigan called Birmingham. Now it a very trendy yuppie upscale area. Back then in was just a nice city with a nice downtown area with many bars & restaurants. It is still very nice it's just changed. There was a bridal store in the downtown area with big windows and mannequins wearing fancy, elegant and expensive wedding gowns. Usually after taking a girlfriend out to dinner we would take a walk around the downtown area. I made sure to walk by the bridal store, stop and look in the window. If I was feeling brave I would tell the girl she would look good in a specific gown. It's funny but whenever I did that my night seemed to go better. I think it planted a seed in their mind that I was marriage material, somewhat serious, had a future plan… I'm a pretty logical person and I stored results in my head. Kind of an a/b comparison. A= we walked by the store and I made a comment, B= We didn't go near the store. In analyzing the results it was very clear that there was some success to be correlated with walking by the store. Today I have further developed this concept. If I stop by a magazine store ( and they are getting harder to find by the day) I pick up some bridal magazine. I give it to the girl I like and tell her I was at the store buying a magazine and I saw this and it made me think of you. Do you like the dress on the cover? Or looking through the magazine what dresses do you like? Often this has had great results. Other times it's backfired, scared girls… Well I have gotten of subject with my stories about getting involved and being serious with girls and especially relationships between owners/managers and dancers. Lets circle back to dancers.

I want to start of this section with a disclaimer, it doesn't apply to all dancers. There are many exceptions. But they are rare. Your typical dancer is a real person, with feelings, thoughts and all of the emotions and characteristics everyone has but is also in the context of normality a MESS! One needs to keep this in mind when recruiting, hiring and managing dancers. They fit into a pattern, this pattern is that they walk to their own pace. They live life on their terms. Typically they have little understanding or care for the real world. They are strippers because they need or like the job. All of them are in it for the money. Where else can a girl with no education, no training, no job experience make thousands of dollars a week? So the first and biggest common denominator is that they are stripping for the money. All of them have different needs for money. Beyond the basic needs of life which many dancers really are oblivious to, dancers have special needs. In a short period of time they realize that there are men that will attempt to or will provide for all of their needs. All they need to do is ask, smile and allude to what might be forthcoming. I know of many girl that have a stable of customers that pay for all of their needs. One pays the rent, another the cell phone bill and on and on. I would say that there is a large portion of dancers that have substance abuse problems and need daily cash to support their habits. Some dancers actually many dancers have legal problems that require large amounts of money to pay off fines, probation, restitution…Many are single mothers with no better way to work a few evenings or afternoons a week to support themselves and their families without working full time and for a lot less money. Many have a significant other, boy friend or husband that they support. So many of them do not drive or have a car. They have traffic infractions, drinking and driving problems, drivers licenses taken away. At the time of the writing of this book there are many "Ride Share" services popping up like Uber and Lyft, these have been a blessing to our industry. With a click on a phone a ride appears quickly and affordably. There is a large pool of dancers that can't work a normal " on the books" job. They are getting some form of government support and the income would disqualify them or they just don't want the financial responsibilities of life and rely on the safety blanket of support.

You also have many what I would call more mainstream dancers. These are girls that see this as a real opportunity to make a living, a means to an end. Often these are college age girls that strip a few days a week to pay for their life and they handle it well. Others are older dancers that have been dancing for a while, know little else or know that this is probably the best course for them and treat this as a real career and work it. These types are an exception.

The final category is new dancers. New meaning they have never danced before. They are recruited via some means to check it out. They may have a friend that dances. They may have come to a club with friends and thought they can do that. Others like the attention and excitement and want to try it out. These new dancers require the most work as a manager but also pay off the best. They are not jaded. They have no previous expectations. Being new they will get all kinds of attention. Some attention is good and some attention is bad. Customers always like new girls, this is good. It will bring in customers, they will stay for a while and the whole cycle of why you have your club goes on. Where it is bad is jealousy with your other dancers. The new girls will get attention, make money possibly take regular customers from another dancer and thus take income from that dancer. So pay special attention to your new dancers, nurture them and make sure they are not picked on by your other dancers.

Logically we know that most people take a job and work because they need and want money. It's important to understand that most dancers have no respect or understanding of money. It's a pretty empowering feeling to make hundreds of dollars in 15 or so minutes. Once this happens the strippers addiction to the business is set in place. Work is measured in good shifts and bad shifts. Financial forecasts in the mind of a stripper are along the lines of " I will have to work Friday, Saturday and Monday so I can pay the rent. It amazes me that most dancers make a great living but have nothing to show for it and no savings or investments. Granted the dancers have expenses in paying the clubs when they work. Dancers go tanning, get their nails done, by clothes and that is fine. But they should put some money away for that proverbial rainy day or bad / slow day. As a manager of these girls it's important that you understand their earning capability in the context of your clubs operation. While it's your goal to be busy every day and night in the real world that is not practical. So a a good manager you understand based on counting your covers and reconciling them with the cctv, looking at your drink sales and your personal observations you know when your slow times are. Guess what your dancers also know this. They will not want to work when it's slow. They want to work when it's jammed and they can make more money. So you need to devise a plan that changes your slow days into busier days and more money days for your girls. Most clubs take a position of punishment to manipulate the girls to work when its slow. Policies like if you want to work a weekend night you also need to work a slow day (insert whatever day is slow) . This work sometimes but even if it works it's a problem. You have a girl coming in on a slow night and not meeting their expectations of earnings. From my perspective you need to increase the profitability of that slow night. The night is slow because people just don't come out as often on a Monday –Wednesday night. So you need to create promotions to bring people in and make that night better. What I have found to work well is a combination of the following things. First we need to keep our main rule in place. We need Dancers and Customers, without both we fail. So create a series of business cards to give out. The first one is for your dancers from you. It will be for ½ off tip out any night within the next 7 days. Sign and date it. What this accomplished for you is your getting full tip out on your slow night where your revenue is off. You are giving away ½ tip out another night and the dancer may use it on another slow night or a busy night . What your really accomplishing is having dancers on a slow night and another night and in reality you are giving up 25% of tip out based on the two nights. Full tip out on the slow night and 50% the second night . And you have at least 2 nights that dancer works. As a practical matter often that card will get lost or not used. Be firm, they need to have the card and use it in the time frame. You can also use this card as a manger any night it's slow and want to perk up a dancer. As an owner, pay attention to the use of this it shouldn't be abused by your managers but used as needed. Your next set of business cards should be an invitation to come to the bar on the slow night and offer free cover.

Rarely do dancers come without drama and issues. It goes with the territory, Rather than fight it, flow with it. This doesn't imply that you shouldn't run your business, have your rules or enforce them. It means pick your battles. This sounds like common sense but so often ego's and tempers flare. The next minute there is friction, animosity and hard feelings. This flows over to everyone and your well oiled machine starts squeaking. Every one of your girls is an asset. They represent a larger choice for your customers. They offer revenue to you with tip out. Most important they contribute to the overall experience of your club.


How do you deal with problematic dancers? Invariably there are going to be problems. Mix competitive dancers with alcohol, "Their" Customers. (some dancers believe that their regulars are owned by them) and their income and there is potential for problems. Many dancers don't drive and rely on rides so they come in late, need to leave early. Many dancers are single mothers that have real problems at times with sick children, ex's and babysitters. Monthly female problems come up. Some dancers like many people have a drinking problem. Others have substance abuse problems. Most dancers worlds revolve around them, that is part of the attraction to dancing. They feel very empowered by the way their customers treat them. Men telling them how exquisite they are, showering them with compliments, gifs and cash can lead to an enlarged head. Finally like anyone else they can just be having a bad day or night. It doesn't matter the size of your club or the number of dancers you have on any given shift the chances are you will have a problematic dancer to deal with.

Unlike  most jobs, dancers really have little accountability or real loyalty to their employers. They know they can always go work somewhere else locally or hit the road. If a club fires them, they still have their phone or address book of customers that are foaming at the mouth to take them out, give them money, take care of them and on and on. When you  fire a girl at your club it has a ripple of effects with positive and negative results. If you feel you need to fire a dancer and you do , it's good. You have eliminated a problem to you. No one likes problems. You have sent a message to your staff that your tough, you won't tolerate problems. On the negative side you may lose that dancers friends that work there. Not always as a result of their loyalty to the dancer that was let go. What happens is the fired dancer goes to work somewhere else. That clubs management like you is always looking for new talent and their customers. So they treat the new girl well. The customers at the new bar check out the new girl and she does well. Dancers talk and socialize as they are a close group. Invariably a conversation ensues where the fired girls talks to her former co-workers and tells them about her new club, the great management and customers and all the money she's making. Logically the other girls go check out the new club and a cycle starts. Customers also follow girls. Most customers have their favorite bar and dancers but also frequent other bars. If their favorite dancer is no longer at your club the customer may go look for that dancer or just go elsewhere. So think through all of the ramifications of your actions prior to firing a dancer. Don't compromise your management style and rules, but think about what you're dealing with and the big picture and the bottom line.

So back to the question of how do you deal with problem dancers? I think each problem and each dancer is different. A schedule with escalating tip out as the shift gets later fixes many problems. A sign in sheet in the DJ booth creates a process of accountability. Whatever the rules are become applied. If a shift starts at a certain time if the dancer is signed in and on stage by the prescribed time , tip out is X, up to 1 hour later it's tip out +$50 and so on. Monthly female problems typically need a few days off, if it becomes a real problem, giving a dancer off until the following Monday, skipping Thursday, Friday and Saturday typically fixes the problem. I used to have a girl that started her period every day when it was slow in the club. I told her to get to a doctor. Kid problems need to be dealt with from a perspective of flexibility and caring. You can't really expect nor would you want to have a dancer not take care of her family. A conversation on the way out explaining that it's important that the dancer resolve whatever issues there are and a follow up call and conversation the next day goes a long way to fixing the problem. Alcohol problems are best dealt with by not allowing the dancer to drink in your club. Drugs are a real problem. Unfortunately they are prevalent with dancers. I'd suggest a no tolerance policy at your club with dancers and customers. Time for a funny story. I was called to my coat check room one night and there was an argument going on with my coat check girl and a customer. He was upset because he alleged someone stole some weed he had in his coat pocket. Anything is possible but knowing the girl it really wasn't likely. So I suggested that anytime we had a crime committed in our club we typically called the police. I picked up the phone in the coat check room and asked the guy what his name was and told him to feel free to wait at the bar until the police came to take a report. He decided not to make a police report and asked me not to call. As for ego's between dancers, issues related to customers you can only try to diffuse the situation by explaining that the customer is the clubs and tell the dancers to get back to work. This doesn't always work. A bad day for anyone is a bad day, just be friendly. Recognize a problem or a potential problem. Be proactive and do your best to be diplomatic. You need dancers to have a men's club.

If you have to let someone go, it's not like in a typical Human Resources situation. Often they can be drunk, high, belligerent and often all 3. Best to just send them home and call them the next day when your both calmer and see where it takes you. If you feel you need to let them go do it then avoiding a issue in front of customers. For some reason I have seen the dismissal of an employee in a club take on a different air then in a normal corporate environment. Sure it's different but it's best to be professional. It avoids so much grief down the road.

As the manager and or owner of a club so much of your time will be devoted to your dancers. It's a fact. The question is how do you use that time? Are you proactive or reactive? Everyone is different and you will need to be both at times. As bad as it sounds a good analogy of the person managing the dancers is a babysitter in a day care / school environment. Some kids play nice by themselves and get along with others. Some kids have fits and temper tantrums. Other kids require tons of attentions. Dancers and kids is interchangeable. In my managements style and as a person, I'm proactive. Not only is each employee important, but they must feel as they are important. The best way to do this is to interact with them. During a six to eight hour shift, find five to ten minutes to talk to them. Remember previous conversations and if need be take notes. A little pep talk to encourage a good shift doesn't hurt. New dancers and employees need more attention. Imagine yourself in a new job, especially a job as a dancer. Not knowing people, not being part of any of the clicks and having to deal with the competitive nature and jealousy of your co workers can make it difficult. The attention of the boss makes these anxieties and real dynamics smoother.

So you opened your club an hour ago. Everything is going pretty smoothly. All of your staff is at work on time and doing their job. Customers are in the club. The DJ has the music flowing focused on the customers taste. All of a sudden you hear some commotion and two dancers having some words. (not nice words) they both feel a customer is theirs. One was sitting with him and go up to go on stage. The other went and sat down with him and made a trip to the VIP area. The dancer that went on stage sees the situation that the second dancer "Stole" her customer and her money. The second dancer may or may have not ever seen the first dancer sitting there, she was just doing her job. To complicate matters it's possible the customer was a "regular" customer of the first dancer. One who comes in to somewhat exclusively see her. How do you diffuse this situation? It's hard. There is merit in both dancers perspective. Further the first dancer who went on stage genuinely sees herself as wronged and has as lawyers might say real damages (she missed the cash in the vip room). Really all you can do here is try to diffuse the situation. You need to explain that this is your club, not the dancers. These are your customers not the dancers. Logically neither girl works every open hour of the club and a customer can come in any time. If the customer really exclusively wanted to see the first dancer he would have told the second dancer that he was waiting for the first dancer, came in to see the first dancer... A common occurrence is dancers mark their territory. They leave a drink, their purse, a towel or something with a customer marking that this customer is theirs. Should this have happened we might treat it differently. Back to the conversation, it's a team effort. There is no room for friction between dancers over customers. The second dancer was doing her job as was the first. Explain to both that the situation could also happen the other way. Buy them both a drink and send them on their way. If it keeps happening with a specific dancer, you need to tell her you appreciate her aggressiveness but we have a team here and she needs to be a team player and she needs to play like the rest of the team.

Dirty girls, extras... Invariably eventually you are going to get a situation where one dancer or a group of dancers will complain that another dancer or group of dancers are dirty. They are engaging in some activity that could range from pulling aside their bottoms and showing their stuff to any degree of touching and outright sexual acts. To my knowledge there are no clubs anywhere in the U.S.A that allow sex in the club between a customer and a dancer. There are varying degrees of permissive nudity , but we will assume here that if there is a complaint it is because the activity is going beyond what is  permitted or expected. I'm going to totally side step the ethical issues of this conversation. As an owner manager you should know and understand many of your customers are coming to your club hoping or knowing that they will have some degree of a sexual experience. What happens is most customers would prefer to have sex or some sexual act rather than a dance. So the girls that do not do extras are forced to compete with the girls that do extras and make little money. Eventually they complain. This is a tough situation. For a little while you can blow it off. It's not like the dancer is having sex in the middle of the stage in front of everyone. You can say you will look into it. Eventually the situation comes to a head. You can talk to the dirty dancers. The first conversation is well I as the manager/owner haven't seen it, I have had some complaints from other dancers that....do me a favor, tone it down and be discrete. It really comes down to your club and what you want to happen. I can't give you advice here, this is a personal decision. The biggest money making clubs that I know of go to either extreme. They are beautiful fancy show clubs with gorgeous dancers that perform and entertain on the stage and extras are a rarity. At the other end of the spectrum the clubs are almost like brothels where girls that do not do extras are the rarity. Then of course you have clubs in between. If this problem comes up, think it through, chart a course and stick to it. Be cognitive of your investment, your license(s) and your reputation and potential criminal issues.

# Operational Considerations

So you have your club, you have your vision and your executing your plan. There are many details you probably never thought of . Lets run through them. It will be difficult to address all of these items specifically because many of them are specific to where your club is located. As an example the hours you are allowed by law to operate. Who you buy your liquor from...I will tell you that as a rule of thumb you will work as many hours as the bar is open when the bar is closed taking care of other things.

**Organization-** you need to be organized. There are so many moving parts and details that it is critical to have some method of keeping track of things. Many people use a computer or phone. These are great tools but can get lost, crash, get stolen... Sure you can use cloud back up. This won't turn into a debate on technology. I suggest you use technology but also use a few books and pens that you keep in your safe. Prior to getting organized you will need the following vendors, suppliers and professional service people.

**Lawyer** – Make sure you are set up properly. It's just a matter of time before you get sued for wrongful termination of employment, some on is involved in a drinking and driving issue, someone hurts themselves or gets hurt in the bar. Different violations serving a minor, staying open to late, dancers not following the local rules. With the best intentions stuff happens. From a business perspective are you better of as a corporation, LLC, separate companies owning the property from the operating business...

**Accountant/CPA** – In this business there is a lot of reporting and taxes. Typically your insurance is based on your sales. You product ordering is very regulated and tracked. Credit card sales are documented. You should have a system where your accountant regularly (at least monthly) meets with you and organizes your books. Payroll needs to be addressed, typically this task is designated to your General Manager signed of on by the owner and called into a payroll company. A time clock is part of this.

**Insurance** – There are many types of insurance you need from liability related to liquor sales, your business fixtures and building... you have a cash business, often an ATM with cash in it. Make sure your policy covers on premise cash in the amount you need as well as transportation to and from the bank. Insurance protection from electrical surges and lightening for your sound and lights system are both areas that often are thought of after the fact.

**Maintenance Contractors** -  The good news is that these type of people will beat a path to your door and be your customers. Grab a business card holder book and store these cards. You never know when you will need someone and having a choice at your fingertips is good. The people you will need regularly beyond the day to day cleaning of your bar are:

   a. Heating and cooling contractor to maintain your furnaces and AC. Regular changing of filters and seasonal switchovers as needed.
   b. Beer/ walk in coolers / syrup $CO_2$ people to maintain your coolers, clean your beer lines and maintain your syrup system. Often it's the people that sell you beer and syrup.
   c. Landscaping – the lawn needs to be cut and the snow removed.

d.  Garbage removal – dumpster try to arrange for a Monday pickup.
e.  Alarm system – Burglar, fire and hold up and Closed Circuit TV people.
f.  Carpet Cleaning – make sure you do this regularly.
g.  Sound and light system maintenance person. You will always be replacing light bulbs, re –aiming…Modern LED lights have eliminated much of this.
h.  An all around maintenance person
i.  An exterminator.

You want to have a system in place where things get taken care of. As an example the carpets get cleaned the first Sunday of every month. Test your Alarm system once a month, the last thing you want to do is hit a hold up button and have the batteries to be dead. Little things like a burned out bulb should be written up every shift and filter in to a to do box in the office for the General Manager to take care of. There is really nothing complicated about the day to day operations of the club, but there are many things that need to be taken care of. The most important thing is the staff, specifically recruiting new dancers. It's part of the business that dancers move on. They get married, get sick, retire and all kinds of other things. We know that for the business to be successful we need dancers. Never stop recruiting, you can never have to many dancers.

Lets talk about an accounting system real quickly. I suggest you get two books. One that is a multi column journal. On the left axis of the page you put the days of the month with a page for every month. On the top axis from right to left you label your columns such as sales, cover, tip out, valet, shots, paid out and total. Thus for every day you fill in the dollar value positive or negative for each column. And at the right side you have a balance of what you should have in cash on hand. You treat Credit Card sales as you like, I do not typically include them in this book only cash. You also get a hard cover yearly journal they are usually red. In this book on each day you take further notes. As an example in the paid out column you might run out of cream for coffee or give an employee an advance. This is where you detail these expenses. I also suggest 2 folders from the office supply store. One with days of the month and on with months. As you have receipts you file them in the days file. At the end of the month the go in that month. You determine how much cash you keep on hand and any excess goes to the owners/bank as directed. This also allows you to quickly see where things are from the sales side of things. Your expenses would be tracked via your online bank payments or checks written.

Now you know how to run a club. You understand the layout of the club. What probably is the most efficient way to lay it out. You have a feel for the employees and their functions. There is a system in place that takes into account the day to day operations of the club. It opens and closes, people are scheduled for work, inventory shows up and is sold. The club is on auto pilot and running. The next step is to always strive to improve your bottom line and be more profitable . You achieve this in two ways.

The first is pretty obvious lower costs and increase revenue. The second and most important detail is to make the club better. Attract more customers and dancers that spend more money. Slow and steady wins the race here. Don't do anything dramatic or radical just keep improving.

Let's talk about marketing. It really doesn't matter if the club is brand new or been there forever. You want to keep your brand out and in the mind of your customers. You also want to attract new customers. Your best way of promoting your club is via your existing customers and dancers. Each one of these people are an ambassador of your club. As an owner or manager it's important to make every customer a VIP and that they should feel important and welcome. Make a point to say hi and shake their hand. I like to ask a customer " Weren't you in here last week with some friends"? If they say yes, ask them where are the friends tonight? If they say no, tell them they should bring their friends. And then hand them a few VIP cards. When they show up with the friends again make your rounds, say hi, buy a round of drinks...Your dancers should be at every home team sporting event dressed to impress wearing something that designates they are from your club, a t shirt, jacket ... They should have vip cards with their name on them. They should be circulating among the crowd and inviting people to the club. A quick wink and a "I'd love to talk to you but I have to get going come see me some time" brings them in. Letting it be known that the after concert/sporting event is at your club and free admission with a ticket stub always helps. Most bands that tour end up somewhere after their concert, why not your club? Whom ever does your promotions should make a point of working this. There is a magazine called Pollstar they publish a directory of talent agencies, managers... They also publish the schedule of most major and minor tours and the venues that the acts are playing act. It takes a little work but pays off to call the agency that represents an act, get the tour managers contact information and call or email and invite them to your club. The girls in person at a show can also do this. It gets a little harder to really apply this but work the tuxedo rental place managers and limo companies for bachelor parties. Make sure they have a stock of vip cards.

Parties, have as many as you can as often as you can. Everyone loves a party! Every dancer has a birthday. There are events every month you can celebrate. Pick a day, advertise it and make it a great event. It will act as a anchor for other events. It will be busy all your staff will want to work, it will bring in customers and grow.

Social Media is really important and an ever changing field. You will find some customer that is a graphic designer builds websites, does social media... Make that person your Executive Vice President of Social Media Promotions. Give them a title, give them a business card, give them a tab and a little money and let them go to work. An important component to social media and your total promotional campaign is to build marketing lists. There is a challenge many people may not want marketing targeted to them because of wife's, girl friends... so you need to ask, keep your messages clean...

With some frequency your customers should be touched with the events that are upcoming, some sort of coupon or incentive that expires to come in. Your facebook page and twitter post should include the events upcoming, some food and drink specials and who is working that day. If you have the right person to work this a racy joke every say Tuesday adds some stickiness to the post. At the same time you DJ and the person that greets people when they come in to the club should be collect names, numbers and email addresses as well as promoting the social media of the club. A great way to get likes on face book is to run it in conjunction with a face book like. Your dj announces in a full bar, does anyone like $ 3 shots? The crowd will answer in affirmation. Your DJ then says any one that shows your waitress that they have liked our face book page gets that special. Of course run whatever special you like.

Mainstream Radio/Cable and local promotional papers seem to be pretty expensive with little results. You can try them. They add to brand awareness but in recent years I don't see the value. If you are going to try I suggest you avoid the expensive premium most desirable time slots and focus on the less expensive timeslots in quantity. Most cities have a newspaper that is geared to adult entertainment. It doesn't hurt to have a presence in these papers.

Anytime you can get some positive press also helps. Most cities have situations where they need volunteers, soup kitchens, holiday meals, cleaning up blighted neighborhoods .. your club's presence or donation is both a nice thing to do and any positive press always helps. Small checks to all local officials election/ re-election campaigns are a good idea. If there is a school local to you, sponsor one of the teams. As we are talking about teams sponsor a softball team or a pool or bowling league. You will always get negative press from people that do not like our industry utilize any and all opportunities to get good press. Don't be phony people will see through that. Just be a productive business located in your community. As an example, if you own your own snow plow and there are houses nearby on occasion especially in a storm, clean up your neighbors drives. They will not forget that. You want people to acknowledge you're a good business even if they don't agree with the nature of your business.

The next area to look at is profitability. Classic thoughts are cut costs and increase margin. This is a good idea but not always easy to execute in a men's club. One very important area to look at that many people neglect is your hours of operation. It's hard to be open 6 days a week from before lunch to late evening / early morning. Might you make more money being open only evenings? Does your day business justify the related costs? Are weeknights really slow? Might closing a Tuesday or Wednesday night or both make sense? When you look at the costs related payroll in a men's clubs it's unlike many other business's as much of your payroll is very minimal and typically the dancers tip out covers it. To operate in negative figures is pretty hard. But this doesn't mean that there is not a cost. Your dancers will despise slow nights. Sure you can have them take the good with the bad, but is it really worth it. Might you be better off bringing in your whole crew less days and making the same amount of money. This isn't an easy answer. Often you might want to start off slowly at a new club with evenings only. Then perhaps add a day shift and keep growing. Or maybe skip lunch and open at 4pm with a happy hour. There is no right or wrong answer. Just look at your numbers and your scheduling and let it speak to the issues.

At a previous point we discussed pricing related to the benefits of lower priced well drinks –v- higher priced premium brands. No need to repeat this. It's easy to raise prices. The common thought is that you have a monopoly, customers want your girls, they don't care about a few extra dollars for cover, drinks...This is partially correct and also is a flawed concept. Most customers have a budget of some sort. They are going out and while this budget isn't fixed in the traditional sense, there is a dollar figure in mind. This customer is typically going to spend the most money on your dancers. If you look at it, does it really matter where you get your money from? I don't care if it comes from liquor sales, food sales, cover or tip out. To me the bottom line is the bottom line. Knowing that the customers are coming in to spend money on dancers, why not encourage this via fair pricing on parking, cover drinks and food and make more money on the use of your vip area and tip outs? If its painless to come in and have a drink more often the dancers will do their job and get their money from their customers. Eventually customers will gravitate to your bar because they don't feel like they are getting mugged going in and there is a good selection of dancers. This will encourage more dancers and more tip out and more vip fees. So if you're at a point where you are thinking you want more revenue look at how to get more tip out and more girls. If you serve food look at your pricing. There is nothing wrong with a $50 surf and turf, but a $5.99 burger and fries and your entertainment is hard to pass up on. Have something for everyone. I'd suggest something on the lighter side to be available also.

You have a unique establishment where you can charge higher prices than usual. But you have competition and customers that have choices. Find the proper way of doing things for your club.

# So you want to date a dancer?

This next section of the book is focused on dancers. I'm going to teach everything I know so you can benefit from my experiences. Dancers have a unique appeal to most men. For starters you can pick what you like. Hair color, ethnicity, size, age, personality, intelligence… it's like a smorgasbord. You have a chance to interact with this woman on your terms typically for the price of admission to the club and maybe a drink and or a meal. You would spend this on a date anyways. I'm not saying every dancer is available. In fact most have at least one significant other. Conversely if you look, you will usually find what you want. So what do you want? You should have this thought through so you have some sort of plan. What you want and your plans will probably change many times but you still should have a plan. To make things pretty simple most people in pursuit of a dancer are looking for at minimum fun with a beautiful woman. There may be a difference of opinion of what is fun, who is beautiful but what is important is that she is beautiful to you and you have fun.

Like any endeavor in life you want to stack the deck as much as possible in your favor. What I mean by this is that you need to understand the world through the eyes of a dancer in order to get beyond knowing her in a professional arrangement as a dancer and you as a customer. Although it doesn't hurt to start as a customer, it's hard to move on and out of this situation and often a dancer just doesn't see you as anything more than a customer. It's kind of like being stuck in a friend zone. Let's look at things first through the eyes of a dancer.

The discussion that follows is speaking in generalities. There are exceptions and not everything applies to everyone. Just think this through and apply it as you see it. Dancing is a job, it is work. People work for money. Some people also enjoy their work others do not. When you go into a club and talk to a dancer, she is working, she is trying to make money. In fact being at a club probably is costing her money. She will always initially see you as a customer as money. You are looking at her as a woman to date she is looking at you as a customer, a source of money and income for her. When there is a disconnect between both of your agendas, probably nothing will happen and probably any future potential will be clouded by the disconnect. There is nothing wrong with telling a dancer you don't want a dance and you don't want to give her money. In fact many will respect that you are not wasting their time. Others might feel slighted that you're not interested. Dancers are people, social animals and most like to interact with other people. Thus if she is not dancing for anyone, if the club is slow there is nothing wrong with you being a friendly person. Keep in mind that most dancers get hit on hundreds of times per week. They have heard it all from how beautiful they are to what each customer can do for them. What is going to get her attention and move you further along in the game towards your goal is her feeling comfort in interacting with you and at least not having any repulsion to you and hopefully some attraction. Taking this a bit further she must perceive you as fitting her view of normal and not being threatening, a pervert …From a repulsion/attraction perspective you should be dressed nicely, not look ragged. You should be clean. There is nothing wrong with getting dirty and working hard. I see guys that work in construction and agriculture coming into the club after work and not cleaning up. It's not a winning strategy. Take a shower, brush your teeth wear clean clothes…Be responsive to her conversation. Meek and indecisive replies to her will get you nowhere. Be interesting, funny, intelligent and give her a reason to talk to you. Take mental notes for the future as you will usually have many conversations. Rarely is it one conversation. Prepare yourself for this adventure.

You have a plan, you're going stripper hunting. Your showered and dressed, you are on a mission and you have picked your club and are on your way! Do you go alone? I have mixed emotions on this. There are benefits and drawbacks to both going alone and going with a friend. Remember you want to be seen as non threatening, normal not a typical customer. Going alone and not being a regular at that club sort of shouts that you are on a mission. Conversely you can diffuse that issue pretty easily. Going with a friend makes you seem more normal. A couple guys going out looking at girls and having some drinks. Going with a friend or group of friends also makes it harder to work on getting to know a dancer. They will approach you and your friend in like numbers. You don't stand on your personal virtues, your looked at as a group, this can be good or bad. Whatever you do is fine. Mix it up and see what works best for you.

At first as your learning this process I'd suggest going alone. Be nice and friendly to everyone. As you enter the club try to get a table for two rather than sitting at the bar or at the side of a stage. Say a friend is meeting you. Learn the layout of the club. Pay attention to the girls on stage, knowing their names and looks will give you some idea later how many girls are working . Once the same girl goes up again it implies that you have seen most of the girls. Some could come in later, others may be in the VIP but you have some idea. Order a drink, tip your waitress and sit back. You are on a reconnaissance mission. The first time you are there you are planting seeds to harvest later. If something interests you make eye contact , enough to have her notice and break it off. You will be approached by many girls. They will all ask you similar questions. What's your name, are you having fun, how long have you been here, have you ever been here before, what do you do, what are you drinking and Finally WOULD YOU LIKE A DANCE or GO TO THE VIP?

How you conduct yourself at that point sets the future up. I like to explain that it's my first time here, it's a nice place… May I buy you a drink? Of course only if you're interested. Avoid any real personal questions beyond what is your name. Avoid general compliments like your beautiful. Compliment her if possible on something unique, nail polish color, jewelry her choice of music. Make it known that you pay attention to detail. She is more than a body with tits and ass. When it comes to if you have ever been here before or do you go to other clubs, I prefer to say I have been but it's really not my thing. Same thing when it come to dances/vip. It's pretty normal to like to go out and have some drinks, look at dancers and have fun. You don't want to make the impression that you're a pervert, a "regular customer" one that buys dances etc. Tell her you would love to in concept get a dance , go to the VIP …but it's not really for you, that you're just going to relax and wait for your friend. She will probably excuse herself say it was nice meeting you…and move on. Eventually a few other dancers may try you. They will talk and ask each other about you and hopefully they will say you were nice but were not getting dances. At some point you leave. Try to say good bye to the girls you were interested in, tell them it was nice meeting them, your friend was a no show… This good bye shouldn't be like leaving a family reunion and saying good bye to a long lost relative. Just an additional acknowledgement and interaction. Keep it light. It was nice meeting you, I'm taking off . They will tell you to come back and see them again, tell them you will. Ask when they are working next and move on.

What you have done is established yourself as a normal person, not a customer. You were nice and polite and deserve future conversations. Try to get back to that club on the same day and time you were in the following week if you want to pursue a dancer you met. Dancers often keep similar schedules. Same drill again  grab your seat and a drink and wait. I said wait, do not chase. Let them come to you. If they don't there is always next time. The conversation with circle back typically to some recognition of you in the past. Refresh their memory, I was here waiting for my friend who ditched me and we hung out. How are you? What have you been up to…Eventually she will get to the dance part again, now it's time to make a decision and investment. Tell her your torn, it sounds like fun but it's not really your thing and you don't want her to look at you as a degenerate pervert customer or whatever word you want to use. Ask her point blank, what is the point? If the chemistry and flirting is there say something along the lines of I hate to start something I can't finish. Or I have enough to think about in my life without thinking about wanting more of you .She will tell you common it will be fun, I won't think badly of you…Go get a dance or two. Reserve this for the one you want, do not get dances from multiple dancers. They will talk and all see you as a customer. Dances can be very mild or aggressive get a few and call it quits. Tell her you had enough you have to be able to sleep tonight. Ask her to get you some ice for the swelling, she will laugh, go back and finish or have another drink. Tell her that is not what you expected. She will ask you what did you expect? Smile and tell her everything is great. Now it's time to pry a little deeper as long as you are not monopolizing her time. If she clearly has a stage name, often I ask her what does her mother call her? Where is she from? Any small talk that is non confrontational, non stalking and not to personal. Wrap it up and say good bye.

Three times is a charm as the saying goes, on your third trip it's time to see where you are at. You have done your homework and put in your time you have made an investment. Your dancer will see you and approach you. Say hi grab a drink and have your small talk. Transition your conversation quickly into your close. Something along the lines of I have really enjoyed getting to know you, been thinking a little about you and I want to get to know you better. I understand that when you're here, you are working, trying to make money and have a job to do. I'll never really get to know you like this. You mentioned you like _____food, there is a great restaurant called _____ not to far from here. Let's have dinner this week is _____ or _____better for you. And stop and see where it takes you. She might say I'd love to but I have a boyfriend. You know where you're at. She may tell you she'd like to but this week, the days you proposed don't work. Immediately counter with asking her what day does work. She may tell you she wants to get to know you better before she sees you outside of the club. This typically is a blow off and a way to try and get more money and dances from you. Cut your losses and move on. The best scenario is she say yes and makes a date. Don't hold your breath the odds are 50-50 she will be a no show. If you get your yes, go get a few more dances, any other scenario move on. Finally you want to ask if she will be meeting you there or should you pick her up? Ask for a phone number in case you can't make it, need directions… When you get the number it becomes time to be a stalker, put it in your search engine of choice, face book … and read all you can. Don't mention you did this, you don't want to appear as a stalker but it never hurts to get some insight into a person. From there use your best manners over dinner keep it light and keep moving forward.

Before we analyze the preceding paragraphs and process's it's important to understand a dancer. You can go back to the previous sections of this book and re-read the parts about recruiting and retaining dancers as employees. Much of this applies. But you have a different agenda and you are in a different place then an employer. There are a few hurdles you will need to get over. The biggest is not being a customer or a financial asset. Dancers also have read this book. In fact they have taught me what I know and am conveying to you. Don't think that because a dancer gave you her number, went out with you and is having sex with you changes her thought process on you as a customer. You are potentially just a different class of customer. Some people as a hobby play golf, others own a boat others like to date strippers all these hobbies come with a cost. Most of these dancers have a stable of customers they date, that "Help" them . Some pay the rent, others the car payment, others the phone bill… Just think, when she asks you for "Help" is this something you want to participate in. Is it for you. If you were married you would help your wife, is this different? When the requests come in for help, you can help or offer alternative solutions. It's all about your budget, desires and results. Typically you have to be a customer, then develop a friendship and relationship, it's a cost of doing business. Just make sure you are objective and it is going along at your pace. The other issue is safety. So many dancers have had bad experiences or have heard about them. They have been drugged and raped or just raped. They have had fans turn into stalkers. So your dancer needs to feel comfortable around you. The best way to accomplish this is to portray normality. Be nice. Don't make lewd remarks. Be a gentleman. When you go out at first make it safe, easy and fun. Nothing over the top. Two schools of thought, it really depends on the person. Stick to something they know and are comfortable with or do something new. As examples, you can always go out to dinner, we all have to eat and it's pretty plain and safe. Going bowling or shooting pool adds a little competitiveness to a date. A comedy club can be fun. Trying something a little different like an ethnic festival, horseback riding, an escape room  something that you don't do often can be fun also. The most important thing is to be light and fun. You want to create a thought process that you are special, different than just a customer. All women want their prince to sweep them of their feet and live happily ever after. When it's over a quick, I enjoyed that, it was fun, see you soon and maybe if she initiates it a hug and kiss and that is it.

No it's time to get this romance of the ground and in to high gear. You have seen this person a few times in the club. You have taken her out once. You have been a gentlemen and fun. In between all of this it's a good idea to send a flirty text maybe once a week, no more. You don't want to appear as they say thirsty, but keep your presence felt. The next step isn't for everyone and a lot depends on your budget. The idea here is to get her away for a vacation , weekend … You can be totally upfront and honest at this point. Pick a location and event and invite her. I'm going camping in a couple of weeks and I'd like you to join me. I'm taking a trip to an amusement park for the weekend I want you to come along it will be fun. What always works is I have a business trip / meeting in (_____ ) Pick a city destination that is interesting and a ways off ) and I want you to join me.  Even if you don't have a meeting just excuse yourself for an hour and come back. Make sure you use the " I want you" not would you like to. Taking that trip with you has all kinds of positive aspects attached to it. It tells you that she has the ability to be with you for a long period of time. Probably no serious live in boyfriend/husband/relationship. It implies a trust between you, she trusts you, to go away with you. It also implies that you will be in a hotel room together and she will get a chance to go beyond teasing you with her dancing…You can run into resistance. She may not trust you yet. She may have a significant other. She may have issues that preclude her from going away, kids, probation, a substance abuse problem or other things. The date you pick could collide with some other thing she has going on. You need to sort this out. The most important thing is to NOT keep going in to her club and getting dances or it will never end and you will always be a customer. Another situation that could come up with a pro dancer is that she will see this as an opportunity to keep you as a customer, to test you, to attempt to extract more money out of you. She will tell you that sounds like a great idea, sounds fun and I'd love to go, except I need to work. I have $ due for my rent, car, probation or a zillion other things. She will ask you to help with these expenses or hope you will respond with let me help you with that. This is a tough choice to make. So much depends on your budget, your desires and what you think will be the outcome. Just know that it usually never stops. I have found that this multi step process works well. You may need to change it around a little to fit your needs and the circumstances. The foundation of this is that you develop a friendship, you overcome trust issues and you achieve your goals.

There are zillions of books, web sites, seminars and discussion groups on how to interact with women. How to date them, There are resources of relationships. None of this implies that anything you know is wrong, that dating is hard or problematic. They just share knowledge. If you look at what you know about women, dating and relationships it's pretty interesting. Think through your first attraction to a woman, your first crush, your first date, your first relationship, your last relationship, your first kiss, your first sexual relationship and on and on. Where did you learn about these things? What examples did you have that made impressions on you. What did you pattern yourself after and who did you emulate? What has worked and not worked? From this frame of personal reference and knowledge, where do you want to go? What do you want to accomplish? Apply this same thought process to your dancer. It gets interesting.

Over the years I have made many friends that frequent men's clubs. When I had my two clubs I had the opportunity to meet and get to know the significant others of many of my dancers. Interestingly enough I have been around this long enough where I have there are dancers that I met when they were in their early twenty's that are now approaching fifty. Many have settled down , got married, had kids, have a normal (non dancing/bar) job. Other are a wreck, mid life with no life except drinking and substance abuse problems. Let's look at what might attract you to a dancer and than what might attract a dancer to you. Understanding this attraction and having real achievable expectations will help set the frame work for your success. You have a different set of expectations and patience for a child than an adult. A similar thought process applies to most dancers. Knowing this will save you all kinds of frustration and make your adventure work.

When I have discussed the attraction to strippers with other men, the most common attraction is sexual. If you think about it the scenario in which you are exposed to a dancers sexuality –v- a regular interaction with a woman it's one hundred and eight degrees opposite. Under normal circumstances you meet a woman and she is wearing clothes. These clothes could be very sexy and revealing. At a beach, pool, gym or in some similar situation she might be wearing a bathing suit. Normally she is dressed with some semblance of modesty. When we go to a strip club the woman eventually is wearing nothing or just a small G String bottom. Normally at a strip club the woman has just come out of the dressing room, her hair and makeup is done. You have a very different opportunity to access and evaluate a woman from the perspective of their physical looks and body. This doesn't happen in real day to day life in such a simple way. In the club situation your dancer is saying at least for the moment I'm a woman that is showing off my body, putting my best foot forward (actually not usually her foot) . I have put on what I think is a sexy outfit, done my hair, nails and make up solely for the purpose of attracting you to me. When she is on stage she is dancing and moving in a way that draws attention to her sexuality. Dancing slowly, touching herself, rolling her hips, doing floor work… Removing her costume. You get the picture. So it's pretty natural and normal to be attracted at a physical / sexual level to a dancer quicker than you might to a woman in any other environment.

A dancer in a club is working. Her work consists of extracting money from you in the way of tips, personal performances and maybe extras. She is a saleswoman selling you on herself and these services. She is trying to distinguish herself from the other dancers and land you prior to someone else getting you and your money. Her sales pitch ranges from the not very effective amateurish "Would you like a dance" to some of the most well thought out approaches I have ever heard. This interaction is the next step of interaction and attraction between you and a dancer beyond and after your visual attraction. What she says, how she says it, her voice, accent, delivery and choice of words make up this phase. There is very little right or wrong here. Although a dancer could be abrasive it's pretty hard to not be open minded and hear what a dancer has to say when she's talking to you. This is also a two way process, she is also interviewing you even if she's not thinking on those terms. How does she move you forward from greeting you to having you give her money. The skill set of dancers is all over the place. She will ask general questions that will  help her sort out how to move forward with you in the club getting money. Her questions will be designed to evaluate your worth to her as a customer. Should she even sit with you , will you be a waste of time or will she take her time thinking that you are the type of customer she is looking for. One that is not of any danger. One that will give her money. The dancer recognizes that all people are different. While she is not typically a formally trained and degreed psychologist or sociologist she has lots of field experience speaking to quantities of people every shift. Hearing their life stories or what they want to tell. Recognize what she is asking you, what it means and formulate your answers with your end goals in mind. This is similar to a job interview. You are dealing typically with a experienced recruiter if you want the job you need to answer the questions correctly.

In this next section I will discuss typical questions and interactions between a dancer and a customer. Look at these questions and answers from both perspectives and what they mean. Think through how you might answer these questions and how your answers will affect the eventual outcome of your conversation.

1. **The greeting**. It will usually be a simple HI. Your affirmative response and then the extent that you reply and the intensity of your reply is relevant. The dancer has made

contact with you, she has said hi. Do you respond back with just a hi? Do you say Hi my name is____what is yours? Do you want to be passive or aggressive here? Do you want to appear shy, aloof, friendly...? At this stage of the game I like to control the conversation. Controlling doesn't mean dominating the conversation. I can learn more at this stage by listening rather than talking. By observing the dancers pattern and response to my answers also tells me all kinds of things. So I'd suggest responding with a warm "HI" some eye contact and a smile.

2. **Joining you**.   You have greeted each other. The next step will be some form of the dancer joining you and engaging you in further conversation. Pay attention if she just sits down without asking permission or your invitation. While not always, it's a sign of aggressiveness, desperation or lack etiquette unless it's immediately followed by some form of the following typical questions. " May I join you,  Are you waiting on someone, would you like some company? These questions apply as long as you're not standing somewhere. The dancers goal here is to at a very basic level see if you can be pitched for money. Are you interested in her. She wants to make sure your not with another dancer or waiting for another dancer. The dancer wants to gauge your level of excitement to her asking if she can join you. Your answer says different things about you. Yes, Sure, OK, Please, Why not all are affirmative answers that give permission and indicate it's ok to sit down. Beyond that they all have different meanings. You may be saying to yourself WTF is this author saying. Is how you answer a simple question like can I sit down of any real relevance? Do these dancers really pay attention to what I say? To a dancer is it black or white, yes or no ? This isn't an easy question to answer and the answer applies to everyone differently. But here is defiantly a subconscious reaction to the words you use and their delivery. To discuss this further, a hand gesture open palmed, face up pointing to the chair universally would be acknowledged as an affirmative response to the question may join you, sit down...It really tells little about you accept you were agreeable to the question. If you said ok there is little emotion and not much for the dancer to think about. If you said "Please" it could indicate politeness and possibly some subservience and desperation. Why not might indicate indecisiveness. Of course is an acknowledgment that you're interested. Small things here, but small things add up to bigger things. Every situation requires the proper answer to get you to where you want to be. The only thing here that is important is that you don't waste your time or the dancers. If you're not interested politely send her on her way. Be aware that she will tell other dancers that you are not interested and other dancers will be observing you.

The moment has arrived. You are in a strip club sitting with a dancer and both of you have an agenda. She is figuring out how to get as much money as she can from you. At the other side of the table you are figuring out how to get into her head, heart, g- string or some combination of these things.  So the conversation will now turn into a getting to know you phase.

**Getting to know you** - First thing here, if you have any interest and let's assume you do because you encouraged and allowed her to sit down you offer her a drink. This accomplishes many things. It reflects you have some manners. It reflects you have some money. Most important it buys a little time and gives you a quick and easy common ground of something to talk about. (the waitress, the service, and what you are both drinking).

**What is your name?** Typically initially you will get some sort of my name is ____and what is your name. If your name is Frederick and you are called Fred or Thomas and you are called Tom... I suggest something like my name is Richard but my friends call me Dick. If her name is clearly a stage name , you can ask how did you pick that name, is there any special significance to it. If you feel that it will not be detrimental in the case where a dancer has a stage name I sometimes ask what does your mother call you?

**Where are you from?** This is a multi faceted question that can have a basis in small talk to evaluating your net worth in a dancers thought process. Depending on the situation and your comfort level you can be pretty ambiguous and say from the west side or something like that. You can name the city or you can say I'm originally from____and I now live in_____. I had a friend Scott that would always tell girls he was from a very affluent part of town and that his house was being re-modeled after a fire and that he was staying in a local hotel. It worked well for him and he often would entertain dancers after work at his hotel. Most areas have urban areas, suburbs and affluent areas. Most dancers recognize their local areas and will start to size you up based on what you say. Others may be concerned that you are from their home city or know people that know them. Usually most dancers try to keep their dancing undercover. Asking the dancer where she is from also leads you to further conversations and planting seeds for the future. Knowing your city helps. So when she says she is from stripper city, you could ask have you ever eaten at xyz restaurant? You can then go on to tell her it's pretty good there or she will tell you that. Down the road it could be a good choice for a date or when parting ways stating maybe I'll see you at xyz sometime. As you are doing your due diligence later on when looking for her on social media it helps to know the city she is from. I find the abundance of dancers come from larger cities that offer inexpensive housing in rental homes, apartments and trailer parks. Others may come from a college town and a few may still live at home with their parents. You can take it even a little further and ask did you grow up there, and explore or if other places are mentioned ask and talk about them. Where you are both from is just another piece in the interchange of conversation between yourselves.

**Do you come here often, Do you go to other clubs, have you been here long?** – All this translates into the dancer sizing you up for her financial gain. Usually these type of questions can be translated from the dancers perspective into does this guy frequent clubs? Does he get dances? Does he get or will he get dances from me? Have you been here long can be thought of from the perspective, did another dancer already get to you before me? Are you ready to spend some money...How you answer these questions sets the stage for right now and the future. What your goals are sort of dictates how you answer these questions. If your just looking for some fun now you take one path, if you're looking for some fun and wanting to explore a relationship you might take a different path. With either goal in mind your going to get some dances and as they say get up close and personal. There is really very little benefit in being crude. You don't want to appear to be a strip club virgin or uptight. On the other hand if they already don't know you there is no reason to be a veteran regular strip club customer. So I find the best way to answer the questions "have you been here before, do you frequent strip clubs", is to say you were here a while back. Sometimes you go out with the guys. Going to the strip club is something fun to do on occasion but not your regular thing. If you feel it's not to gushy you might say I'm glad I stopped by today because I got to meet you..

**Do you get dances?** I find it's best to answer "not usually, what's the point". This turns the tables around to the dancer. "Not usually" implies you have, you might. "What's the point"? Puts the dancer in a position to tell you about her dances. An interesting tactic that can work is to say: "It sounds like fun but I don't usually date girls that have danced for me". Let it sink in. She's not dating you (yet). She will get it or ask you about it, what do you mean? You can then explain that while you haven't figured it out yet, there is something different about her, you want to get to know her on a personal not professional basis and she may have a habit of not dating customers and you don't want to handicap or exclude yourself before you get to know her. After all of this she's probably in a different state of mind and is confused, intrigued or pissed off over maybe a little of all 3. Look her in the eyes and speak very softly. Make her lean in and strain to hear you. Using your own words and phrases that fit her level of understand you can qualify what your going to do with anything from saying what the f**k to while it's against my better judgment I took up a little of your time, you need to make a living let's go get a couple of dances. You can than joke around a little and tell your waitress if you're not back in a few songs to come looking for you. You can ask the dancer are you sure this is a good idea? You want to do this…

**How you should conduct yourself when getting a dance** Let her lead. Naturally look her over and check her out but your eyes should make extended eye contact with her. Keep your hands to yourself unless invited to do otherwise. Keep track of the number of dances. After a few call it quits. Unless she offers extras and you want them See post dance later in this section

**Extras -** Extras= sex. It happens all the time. Usually the club offers the use of a VIP area for a fee and what you negotiate for or get extorted for is what you pay. I'm going to spend a little time on this subject because many people are really intrigued by it. Intrigued not really by the sex, but the sex in a club with a dancer. There are many advantageous to this situation. The first is for the most part it's safe. You're not going to get hit over the head. I have seen broken eye glasses and bloody noses when a enhanced dancer gets carried away with her chest on a customer's face. Back to being serious there is a certain level of understanding between customers, clubs and their employees and dancers of what is permissive in an unspoken way. If sex is happening in a club, it's usually pretty low key and drama free. The next advantage is you know to a certain degree what you're getting. If you want a tall girl, a thick girl a blond... you pick out what you like. Finally you have the ability to negotiate and script what you want and what you are willing to pay. If it's your plans to have sex at a club, come prepared. Know your budget and have cash, bring your own condom's and some baby wipes in a zip lock always are handy. Dancers that do extras in my experience fall in to a few categories. Some are professional, they need the money are comfortable in what they are doing , they know what is expected of them, they provide a good experience hoping for repeat regular business. They may test you in seeing how much they can get from you, ask for a tip... But usually what you have discussed is what you get and what you pay for. This brings up an important point. Discuss before you even head to a vip area. This can create a awkward situation. To start off with the dancers always are doing something wrong. Sex for money = prostitution and that's is never allowed legally in a strip club. You being a new unknown person them raises suspicion by asking for specific sex acts for specific prices. Your dancer is going to initially speak in generalities, " you will have fun, you will be satisfied, I'm very hands on" You can ask what do you charge for this, they will typically ask you what are you looking to spend and it becomes a back and forth unproductive conversation. Often they will say lets go in the vip get a dance, I'm very friendly and see where it takes us. So many men in this situation in the vip , having had a few drinks with a beautiful naked girl don't think logically. Then you have the question of are you also paying at the same time a per song fee? Often the dancer will tell you I need to give the dj $ to skip me so we can have fun and he won't call me. I need to slip the bouncer $ to leave us alone. If it's not going the way you want it to , just tell her " you are probably worth a million dollars or whatever she asked for But that's out of my price range, I'm just going to have to dream about you. This usually will bring her back to what can you afford. Know that whatever you offer she will come back and ask for a little more. In speaking to many patrons and dancers that partake in extras. The magic figure usually falls between $100 and $300. Most dancers don't want to get dirty for less than $100 and most patrons can call a escort for $200-$300 so there is a meeting of the minds and bodies in that price range. Earlier I mentioned two kinds of dancers, we have spoken about the professional ones, what is left over are the problem children. They range from scammers that will miscount songs and try to over charge you to girls that don't give you what you agreed upon to pick pockets and more. If you partake in these type of things you will get you experience and some bad experiences go with the territory.

**What is the logical progression after you have received a dance and/or extras?** First you want to be appreciative and fun and then polite and professional. Tell her that was great, you like the way she did_____. She smells great, her hair is soft, you could get used to that. You wish you were at your home with her on your couch...Help her get dressed if it's appropriate. DO NOT make her ask you for money! Diplomatically slip it to her. This is a great time to ask her for her phone number. Just let her know you really liked that. You are need to see her again real soon. Ask when she works next. Often she will offer you her number at that point. If not ask her for it. Tell her it's not like you to come to clubs often and you don't just want to pop in hoping she will be working. Ask can I call you and see if your working…Depending on your comfort level you can ask her to call your phone right than and there. But remember she than has your number. This can tell you a little. What type of phone does she have nice or cheapo. The screen photo if she shows you can be revealing. Hopefully you get her number. Ask should you call , text…? Once you have the number and ask can you call or text it's reasonable to throw in there I don't know if you have a boyfriend or husband…and don't want to cause any problems. Your demonstrating you can be trusted and your thoughtful. Her response can tell you things also. If she says she doesn't smile, tell her your glad to hear that. A quick text that night telling her you were thinking about her you enjoyed meeting her and are looking forward to seeing her soon is nice. Nothing long or romantic just the facts. Let he know you have some balls, you can say what you think … Her response or lack of one gives you further direction.

Lets look at the situation where you got some extras and want more. It's really easy to say you enjoyed yourself and you want more. Just ask if you can see her outside of the club. Tell her it was fun but it would be even more fun in a bed, with more time…She may want to get more comfortable with you. See where it takes you.

One thing that is critical here is that if you are looking for anything more than being a customer, you need to quit being a customer ASAP! Otherwise it gets harder and harder to break out from being a customer. How do you do this? There is an element of timing. You need to be a customer long enough for a dancer to trust you. Trust meaning to know your safe. This needs to be balanced with your positive attributes outweighing the dancer seeing you as a financial asset. When you feel the timing is right, it's easiest and best to just tell her how it is. You can say something along the lines of I like you and want a normal friendship and relationship. I know you have a job to do and need money and when it's you and me I'll always do my best, but for now let's work on it being us. Let's go away this weekend and talk about this and think it through… You will lose some like this but it's a numbers game. Keep at it and you will get what you want.

**Some additional insight into dancers** – while they are people they are a special breed of people. Very unique and different than most other females. They hold a unique power over most men. The dancers operate in an environment that by design places them in apposition of power and esteem. There is nothing wrong with a powerful woman that has self confidence, intelligence and beauty. It becomes problematic when a woman lack all or most of these qualities and is still pursued and complimented by men around the clock. It makes for an unnatural thought process of men. If you're going to have a relationship with a dancer, expect to be thought of as one of these men until you really prove via a history that you are not. Again give any woman the credit she deserves for her attributes and accomplishments but not because your drunk and she's hot and you want her. Many dancers have a substance or alcohol abuse problem. You probably can't fix this. At best you can maybe manage the problem. Typically these are addicts that became dancers, not dancers that became addicts. Go into this with open eyes. Financially most dancers are a wreck. Their money comes very easily to them and they spend it just as easily. Their thought process is I can always work a double shift or make more money tomorrow. They will expect you to pay for everything. Not that this is bad just know it  especially if you have limited means. Not being rich or famous doesn't exclude you. In fact most rich or famous people really have little to do with dancers. Just keep things real. If your luck maybe she will start paying for your things. Understand her schedule and life. A typical 9-5 workday doesn't exist. She will be out until the clubs close, at best and many will hit the after hours, go out to eat and get home when most people are getting up. This isn't all bad . Some of my fondest life experiences was when I was dating a dancer that would get to my house and wake me up in a special way ☺ I would then grab a shower and breakfast and head to work. She would sleep all day. I'd get home and spend a few hours with her before she went to work. Understand that her friends are mainly other dancers and bar employees that keep her schedule. You need to be thick skinned and trusting. Her job is flirting with men and making them want her and to pay her. For most men being that secure is tough enough. Having a girlfriend that does extras is beyond my understanding personally. Beyond some of these quirks dancers are like anyone else. They have their good and bad points. It's been very interesting to see the progression in the lives of many dancers I have known for 10-20 years. Some have maintained the same crazy life style. Unfortunately a few have died. Some have started families that didn't work out. Many others are happily married and reflect back on their dancing time as being young and crazy. I see some of the guys I have known over the years from the bars often at the bars. We reminisce about old times and what happened to…So much has changed but is still the same

The best advice I can give you about dating and getting involved with a stripper is they are people. Stripping is usually not their true personality. The are actors acting. Get to know them for who they are. If you want a stripper because she is a stripper that's fine. But that thought process doesn't make for a good relationship. Conversely most strippers will become great significant others, There is an old saying, you can take the girl out of the bar, but you can't take the bar out of the girl! Enjoy!

# Some Advice to Dancers

This advice comes from me both as an owner and operator of clubs as well as being a customer. If you can't tell by now I like the industry and the people in it. I understand the world as you see it and through your eyes. What I can tell you is be a good dancer, be professional. Come to work to work. Don't sit at the bar or hide in the dressing room. You really need only one customer to make your night and you never know who that person is. Look your best. Do your hair, makeup and nails. Invest in your business. Have a few clean costumes that flatter your looks. On stage, engage the room. Look everyone in the eyes and smile. Tip your dj and have him or her talk you up. When you work the room don't just run around from table to table asking "Do you want a dance"? Be known for being friendly and talkative. One thing that amazes me is that every industry, every business covets and develops their list of customers. Most dancers do not understand this. So many customers just want a friend that is a dancer. A break from their routine. Something exciting. You are their celebrity. The cost of a phone and service is cheap. In fact there are application for most phones that give you a second number. Get one of these and tell anyone that asks you for your number you usually don't do this but here is my number. Make appoint of taking an hour a day and texting your customers. Develop a bond and friendship it will pay off in large amounts of money for you. Ask your manager for some vip passes. Make sure you are an ambassador of your club give these out. Do not chase away new girls. In the short run they may be a threat and take away some business. In the long run they will make the club a better busier place that will allow you to make more money. Balance being friendly with being private with your co workers. You want people to say she's nice , comes in does her job and leaves. No need to get caught up in politics and drama. Finally be smart with your money. You will make tons of it and it's easy to blow. Later on you will wish you kept it. For now you can always go in and make some more. Eventually you will need or want to move on to something else. Consider getting a degree while stripping the flexibility of your job and the money you earn will allow you to do this easily. Stay away from drugs and drinking. If you want to drink make sure you have a safe ride home. Most customers are harmless but don't take chances be safe.

# Stories from the club

These are some of my favorite stories. They are in no special order. I hope you find them entertaining.

I was at my usual hangout, Centerfold in Detroit. It was a late Saturday night. The bar was extremely busy and crowded. Centerfold is known for loud rock and roll I didn't catch the start of the problem but a couple of guys were being asked to leave the bar. The way the bar is set up there is a pretty narrow hallway that leads from the main bar area to the vestibule and then the exit. If tempers escalated it was easy get caught up in the middle of things if you were near the exit and I was. So I decided it would be easier for me to step outside instead of trying to go deeper into the bar and through the altercation. Eventually there were some words and the guys got in their van and squealed their wheels and as they were leaving one of them pointed what at first appeared to be a gun out the window at Jimmy the clubs manager. It was the wrong thing to do for many reasons but the most relevant reason is that Jimmy always carries a gun or two or three and shoots back. So Jimmy pulls his gun out and takes a couple of shots at he van and they speed away. On of the owners of the bar whom is referred to as Uncle George as he is also the Uncle of the operating owner of the bar was telling Jimmy that it's not nice to shoot at customers. We rarely let Jimmy live this down.

Another hot summer night it was around midnight and a bunch of us were sitting around at a picnic table in the parking lot at Centerfold. Valet parking wasn't an option at Centerfold, you self parked and paid an attendant a couple of bucks for watching you car. The attendant sat outside at the table. Smoking in bars was allowed back then and often people came outside to get some fresh air. If you were waiting on a ride or a to go order it was the place to sit. Recently a new fast food hamburger chain called Ralley's opened up about a mile away and everyone liked it and often someone would ask everyone if they wanted anything and someone would make a run to get food..So on this night Z as we called him as his last name started with a Z ran the errand. Z is a really nice guy. Pretty quiet , a little awkward/shy around women and a little gullible but very nice and really wanted to please everyone. He was a regular at the bar and well known. Getting back to the story he went to the place got the orders and came back and left his food on the picnic table outside and went into to give the people inside their orders. Alex another manager who was working the lot that night decided to play a joke on Z and took his hot burger out of the bag and substituted it for a cold burger that was in the walk in cooler from earlier in the day. Z came out and took a bite of his burger and said WTF this is cold. We the proceeded to spur him on and that he should take it back and get a new hot one. He did and we were cracking up. Imaging working at the burger place and making a big order around midnight and this guy coming back with one cold burger. They gave him a new one and to this day if he goes out for food we remind him to make sure it's hot.

At centerfold there were many bachelor parties. Francis who is in my opinion one of the greatest DJ's I have ever heard on the microphone used to have a great technique in conjunction with the bachelors friends. As the bachelor was on stage and being danced for by 20-30 dancers he would abruptly kill the music and tell the bachelor that he has a phone call and one of the bouncers would bring him a cordless phone. Francis would say the call is from the bachelors fiancé naming her by name. Of course she wasn't on the call and he would say they must have been disconnected  but if she calls back I'll tell her you are busy... It got some great reactions.

One night a bunch of us came back from going out to eat and there was a puppy under the dumpster at Centerfold. Sheila gave the dog  some leftovers. The next night or a few nights later I don't remember Sheila decided to rescue the doh. She named her Cody, the dog was Husky Doberman mix. You could see both breeds clearly. Imagine a Doberman with blue eyes a curly tail and the fur of a husky. Cody turned out to be a great dog. Years later when Sheila took an extended trip to Texas she left Cody with me to watch her. She eventually gave me Cody and she was a great dog.

This next grouping of stories relate to a period of time when I had a club called The Wild Goose. This was a great experience. We took a gay men's club and turned it into a wildly successful topless bar. I knew I was in for an adventure from the start. My friend Ron called me one day and said he had a lead on a bar and was I interested and lets go look it over. On the way there Ron explained the situation al little to me. He was funny and concerned  that someone he might know would see him in a gay club, So I told him you should really ask them what they are doing there, we are looking at it as a topless bar. Then he asked me what if some guy starts hitting on him? I suggested he tell him that he is very committed. Ron was a very straight laced, sharp businessman. He negotiated a great deal for us and pretty quickly we were up and running. At the end of the day the numbers didn't support closing on the deal but it was profitable and fun while we were there. These stories are from the Goose as we lovingly called it.

Opening night was a zoo. We had invited everyone we knew and told them to bring everyone they knew. I invited every dancer I knew and told them to bring their friends. We in no way could have anticipated the crowd and we were not prepared for it.  I was behind the bar helping the bartender. It was one of the few places where you could move. Some girl ordered a Russian so I made her one, Rum Kaluha and Cream. She tasted it and said it was good but different. How did I make it and I told her. She then told me usually it's Vodka Kaluha and Cream. I didn't want to embarrass myself so I told her I thought she ordered it Jamaican style. It took off and people started ordering Jamaican style white Russians. At some point I ran out of something I forgot what it was. My liquor storage was in my office. A friend of mine named Peter had previously asked me could he use my office he had to have an important conversation with a dancer in private. I went downstairs to my office and the door was locked from the inside. I Banged on the door and Peter told me he was busy. Nice guy. I told him to grab me what I needed. Our couple of dry runs could have never prepared us for opening night.

I used to hire girls as waitresses, shot girls and coat check girls. They did all three things. If one didn't show it was easy to eliminate the shot girl function or for a doorman to take cover. One night I get a call from the coat check room and the girl tells me she was looking at the schedule and that I'm never going to get into her pants if I always put her in the coat check room. I told her there must have been a mistake in the schedule, to ask the doorman to take cover and come downstairs and let's look at the schedule.

They way I had our phone system set up the last line of the phone system was shared by the pay phone and alarm system. One night I grabbed that line and surprisingly enough there was a dancer of mine who must have been using the pay phone telling her babysitter " to call the club and say that her son is sick and she needs to come home" She was complaining that it was dead, she wasn't making any money...I waited a bit and called the girl down to my office. I told her that her babysitter called and that her son was feeling much better but to please pick up some milk on the way home. The look on her face was priceless.

At one point we built a little vip area in the back of the bar. It was separated by a glass block wall that came up about 4 feet. The idea was to make the are special and to provide a little more privacy. Some dancer, I forgot who had her hands on the wall and was dancing for a customer and the wall came apart. The DJ immediately made a joke about it and suggested no one take her home or near a head board.

I used to have a customer, I forgot his name that would come in every night and get foaming at the mouth drunk. He was a nice guy, not mean or anything just liked to drink to much. I was really worried that he would leave the bar and hurt himself or someone. So I made a deal with him. He would deposit his car keys with the bar. After we closed he would stock all the coolers, take out all the empties and help clean up and have a few cups of coffee before leaving. It worked out pretty good. He sobered up and I had some extra help.

One day one of my favorite dancers Tawny/Cindy was on stage and some guy runs up to the stage and is spitting at her, swearing at her and she is swearing back at him. The bar was pretty busy and I didn't want to ruin the mood and momentum we had going on by grabbing him throwing him out, getting in a fight… So I just grabbed his arm and asked him to come talk to me. We sat at the bar, I bought him a drink and asked him what was going on and what would he do if he was me. I told him you can't come in to my bar and act that way. He was apologetic, explained she was his girl friend and that she did something and was mad. I forgot what it was but it was something really stupid like using up his favorite cereal or something. He went home and that was the last I heard of issues. Tawny also liked small bottles of beer better than larger ones because they tasted better.


Speaking of beer. I had an interesting problem manifest itself to often for me to ignore it. Customers kept telling me that the waitress was taking their unfinished full beers. I asked the waitresses and they seemed confused and denied this was going on. So I was getting sick of giving away free beers. The next tme it happened I went to the closed circuit tv and had a great laugh. One of my dancers Kayla who was under age and we wouldn't allow to drink would just walk by a table and grab a beer, down it and get rid of the bottle. We had a talk and it stopped happening. Kayla was great. When we were getting ready to close at night and the bar was full of regulars she would tell the doorman to lock the door and hold her g string for her and do a set bottomless. The other dancers hated her as she was a tough act to follow.

When we opened it was a pretty tight knit group of people. I would open a bottle of asti and pour all the girls a glass. My wholesale cost was inexpensive, the girls felt special as we toasted to a good night and they didn't get messed up. On night a girl named Cristi came in noticeably late. In the beginning I was pretty strict about being on time. So I figured I would say something and said it in front of all the girls sitting at the bar trying to set an example. She was very apologetic and said she was sorry. She had made a few trays of lasagna in case we were hungry and it took her a little longer than she thought. I felt bad.

I learned a little about dancer politics and being the boss. There was a girl that till this day still makes me crazy. At the time Mercedes was what my dreams were made of. She was smart and crazy. When I say crazy it was in a good way. She was creative and the world revolved around her not the other way around. I like all different variations of women. Mercedes was perfection for her body type. 5"7' of pure toned woman. Long legs, a slender waist, great hips and ass. Perfect natural breasts. A gorgeous smile with perfect white teeth, great lips and deep expressive eyes. She could be a tom boy and wasn't afraid to get dirty. In fact she also worked for her father who owned a shop that cast parts for the automotive industry. I would visit her there and she would be so cute all messed up and dirty. Her father is a hell of a nice guy also. Her brother at the time was old enough to drive but not old enough to legally come into the bar. Of course I treated him special, he would come in with his friends, my valets and doormen knew him and would usher him right in and take care of him. Mercedes at one point was a dancer and I didn't really want her dancing at my bar. She became a bartender. I let her come and go as she wanted and it caused all kinds of friction with my staff but I didn't care. I wasn't thinking clearly. In the end she has been through multiple relationships but always stayed in touch with me. Recently she got married. I hope she is happy. Don't do what I did it's not good for business.

One day one of my dancers came up to me in a panic. She told me do you see that guy over there? You need to throw him out. I asked her why? She told me he was saying all kinds of crude things to her, he wanted to f**k her, tie her up… I told her I'll talk to him. I called him over to the bar, bought him a drink and we talked. I told him the girl liked him but was afraid of him. You can't just come in here and talk like that it won't work. Get to know the girls, buy some drinks let them get to know you. He turned out to ban an all right guy> I would laugh every time I would see him talking to one of our dancers.

One of my favorite stories took place during the auto show. This is a big event in Detroit and we always have all kinds of executives from the auto industry in town from all over and visiting the club. One of these guys gave one of my dancers the key to his room. She told him to go back to the hotel, clean up get in bed.... She would be there later. She then gave the key to another customer and told him she was staying there and to come see her later. I don't know what ever happened but I can't imagine it was good.

There are many other stories but these stick out in my mind. I plan to eventually write an updated version of this book with interviews of people in the industry, formerly in the industry and customers. If you bought this book make sure you like our facebook page so we can stay in touch and you can get the new edition at a special price.

My friend Francis used to tell the crowd at the end of the night you don't have to go home but you can't stay here. Everything sort of has an ending and this version of this book is at its end. I hope you enjoyed reading it.

If you happen to have the chance to get involved in ownership of a club or even to work in one I'd urge you to go for it. This is a unique industry that everyone should experience if they can. While it's an expensive investment that has many pitfalls the upside is amazing. It will never go out of style or get outdated. Men will always chase women. Dancers will always want to work and need money. The trick is to bring all the moving pieces together and have them moving in some semblance of order. What I find to be the biggest downfall or mistake in the industry is the lack of understanding of the business by its owners and what message they delegate to their help. Your core and only business is dancers. Nothing else matters. If you have dancers everything else will take care of itself and you will make money. If you do not have dancers you will struggle. Dancers are a pain, the need to be babysat and managed properly. If you can master this you're in great shape.

If you want to date a dancer you should. Just be aware of what you are getting into. All people are different. No two are the same. I have attempted to give you some insight based on my experiences. Use this as a frame of reference rather than a definitive black and white exact formula to follow. Always remember that a dancers job is to separate you from your money. No matter what entertainment you choose typically there is a cost to it. This is no different. Be safe and use your big head. Dancers are like any other woman out there, treat them properly and you should be successful.

Feel free to post comments on our facebook page. Ask questions as well as answer them. Thanks for buying this book and I truly hope you benefit from it.

www.ingramcontent.com/pod-product-compliance
Lightning Source LLC
Chambersburg PA
CBHW021415170526
45164CB00002B/663